~~CRACKING~~
THE CAMPUS CODE

~~CRACKING~~ THE CAMPUS CODE

Authored by
KARTHICK SEKAR

Disclaimer

This book has been published with all reasonable efforts taken to make the material error-free after the consent of the author. This book is sold subject to the condition that it shall not, by way of trade or otherwise, be lent, resold, or otherwise circulated without the copyright owner's prior written consent in any form of binding or cover other than that in which it is published and without a similar condition including this condition being imposed on the subsequent purchaser and without limiting the rights under copyright reserved above, no part of this publication maybe reproduced, stored in or introduced into a retrieval system or transmitted in any form or by any other means without the permission of the copyright owner.

Registered Office- 907-Sneh Nagar, Sapna Sangeeta Road,
Agrasen Square, Indore – 452001 (M.P.), India
Website: http://www.wingspublication.com
Email: mybook@wingspublication.com

First Published by WINGS PUBLICATION 2020
Copyright © Karthick Sekar 2020

Title: CRACKING THE CAMPUS CODE
Price: INR 599 /$ 9
All Rights Reserved.
ISBN 978-81-947142-1-7

LIMITS OF LIABILITY/DISCLAIMER OF WARRANTY

Dedication

This Book is dedicated
To College Life and College Students

Dedication

Writing a book is an incredibly wonderful journey. This journey wouldn't have been fulfilling if not for some amazing people in my life. It's only appropriate that I give my thanks:

To my awesome Dad, G T Sekar. Dad, you gave me life and taught me how to live. You encouraged me to dream big and follow my heart. You are my hero. You are my biggest inspiration and will always continue to be.

To my Mom, Malaa. Mom, thank you for the wonderful gift of life and all the love and care you continue to shower on me. You have always believed in me and no other blessing in my life can parallel your presence. Without your love, I would be much poorer.

To my Sister, Sasi and Brother-in-law, Siva. You guys are there for me whenever the going gets tough. Thank you for helping me weather the storm during uncertain times. You are always a source of great strength and energy.

To my Wife, Dhivya. You have always stood by me in all the big decisions I have made, knowing very well how crazy they are. Thank you for believing in me and taking care of our little one so I get time for my creative process. Cheers for the partnership.

To my Aunt, Kalaivani. You are the most courageous woman I know and I have always admired your positive attitude. You are the first published author in our family and that inspired me to put my ideas on paper. Thank you for the invaluable guidance in the book-writing journey. Your presence is always a boon.

To my in-laws, Seethapathy uncle, Mathi aunty and Revathi. Thank

you for taking care of me and making me feel at home during

the lockdown. Without your infectious energy, positive vibes and late-night coffee, this book would not have been possible.

To my Nephew, Vasav. You bring out the child in me. You inspire me to stay curious. You inspire me to get imaginative and more importantly, you inspire me to dream... again.

To my niece, Rithika. You make me realize beauty lies in simplicity and happiness is in the little things. You amaze me, every single time.

To my friends Varun, Rahul, Anto and Selva. You always believe I am capable of achieving much more and destined for great heights. Thanks for the constant encouragement.

To my mentors and publishers, Kailash Pinjani and Deepak Parbat. You gave wings to my long-time dream, brought out the writer in me and mentored me through the entire process. This book wouldn't have been possible without your guidance.

To all my trainers, coaches and mentors at various junctures in my life. Thank you for believing in me and providing opportunities to showcase my skills.

And last, but by absolutely no means the least, to my baby boy, Yuvan. It is so thoughtful of you to sleep while I was writing and play with me when I have writer's block. You inspire me.

Introduction

Remember the very first day of your college. From the time you were about to finish your school, you have been dreaming about your college life. The very thought of college life is fascinating. You picture the gang of your close friends, the long drives, the never-ending chats, the gully cricket with paper balls and exam pads, the yummy food at cafeterias and loads and loads of fun. No wonder, college life is considered to be the best phase of anyone's life. This is the image that most of the Indian movies have provided us.

You take that first step into your college campus with a million dreams. The first few days live up perfectly to your expectations. You develop great friendships. There is absolutely no pressure to perform and everything is rosy. You just do not want your college life to end. You hang out at your favourite eating joints, visit nearby places and are having the time of your life. You learn a lot of new things as well.

Just when you think, it can't get any better, things start to take a U-turn. It starts to change slowly but surely. By the end of the first-year, college life is not the fun fantasy you have been living anymore. The singing and dancing routines take a back seat. There are exams to pass and projects to submit. As you get through them and approach the final year, panic sets in. Your only thought is to get placed on campus and land a job. If that doesn't happen, you want to be fit and ready for the battle when you step out of college. Some of your mates get placed in the campus recruitment drives and suddenly there is peer pressure. You start to wonder about your future. Yet, I say again, college life is the best phase in the lives of most people. Today's work environment provides much tougher challenges.

Amidst all this, you see a few of your friends sail through college life with such ease and grace. For a select few, it is just a walk in

share my learnings and experiences with all you college students. I sincerely believe it will help you build confidence, enhance your communication skills and enable you to sail through your college life successfully. I truly believe these skills will also help you build great relationships in your college life and outside of it as well.

How was this book written?

I am a big fan of movies and the part I enjoy most about them is the chemistry that the actors create with each other. Be it the equation between the lead characters or the friendships they portray, I would analyse what worked between them and what didn't. I was always attracted to the way communication works between two human beings. It is the very essence of relationship.

I conversed with a lot of my fellow trainers on the essential qualities required to land 'that' dream job. I picked up the minds of a lot of people in the HR and recruitment industries on what exactly do they look for while hiring a candidate. I discussed with hundreds of students on what worked for them and what didn't in their interviews. I have compiled all those learnings and combined them with my own analysis of my personal experiences.

Nine years as a support executive in the IT department working for various clients around the globe made me realize the importance of being street smart with communication. Five years as a soft skills trainer in several colleges gave me an insight into the mindset of the students and what exactly do they require to crack the campus code.

What's In It For Me (WIIFM)

In the midst of the avalanche of FM channels available on the radio, our favourite FM is always the WIIFM - What's In It For

Me? In fact, every sale, every negotiation and more importantly,

the park. They radiate remarkable confidence whenever you see them. They are the ones who score the best marks. They are the ones representing the college cricket team and they are the ones playing the guitar in inter-college cultural fests. It doesn't end with that. They are the ones who land the best jobs on-campus. You wonder if they have some magic within them. You convince yourself they have some strange power that helps them attract everything they want. You resign yourself to fate believing they are born with some special skills which you do not possess.

Purpose of this book

If you have ever felt helpless at times during your college journey, stop worrying. You are not alone. I was one such student in my college life. Aside from all the fun I had with my wonderful friends, I was always amazed at how some of my college mates got the cream of the cake every single time. They are the ones who topped the class. The select few easily cracked every single interview they attended. They were the most popular ones in college. Everyone wanted to be friends with that elite few.

I finished college, still unable to crack the secret code. I was lucky enough to get placed on campus in a wonderful organization. I had two months of training on transitioning from campus to corporate life. Fortunately for me, my trainers were the best in business. It was on the job that I actually learnt the tricks of the trade of being a magnetic personality. I realized, creating a 'connect' with people is actually not magic.

In fact, there is absolutely nothing that happens by chance. It's a series of strategic steps that the popular personalities follow that make them what they are. Those strategies have helped me immensely in my personal and professional growth. This book is written to

every job interview is based on how it can be beneficial for all the parties involved. The strategies discussed in this book will help you understand the nuances of communication. It will give you the power to convince and negotiate with fellow human beings. It will give you insights on writing a winning resume. It will give you an idea of how to dress up for your interviews and why that can be a game-changer. You will discover proven ways of getting yourself prepared for interviews. You will also understand the psychology behind a few of the most frequently asked questions in personal interviews.

Let's delve deep into the strategies that will help you crack your interviews and land your dream job. Without much further ado, let's get to cracking the campus code.

Index

PART ONE

THE INNER GAME

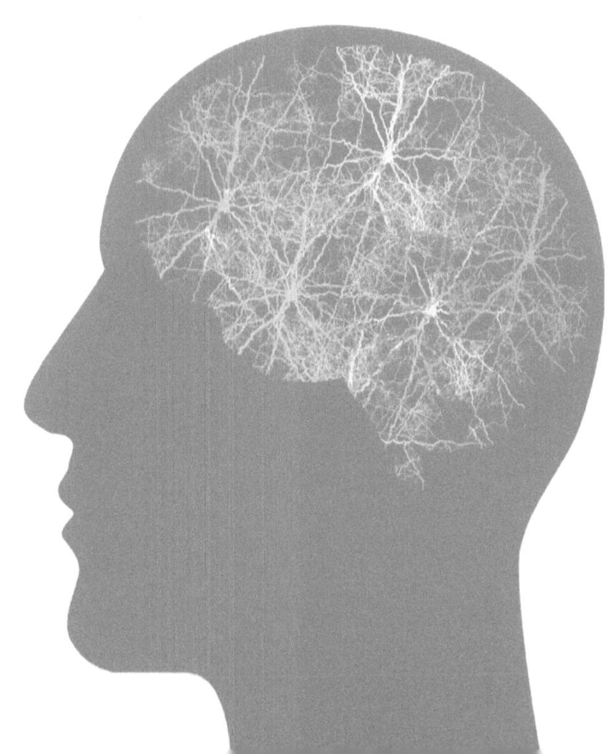

CHAPTER
One
COMMUNICATION SKILLS

All the skills we require to be successful can be divided into two- skills required to build your inner game and those required to conquer the outer game. Simply put, the inner game prepares you mentally for the tough challenges the world will throw at you. The outer game deals with the strategies and techniques that convinces the outside world of your strengths.

I have quite literally taken hundreds of sessions for college students on Personal Interviews. The very first question I ask the students is,

"What do you think are the skills required to be successful at personal interviews?"

Without any exceptions, the first and immediate response would be 'Communication Skills'. Well, no prizes for guessing that. We are very familiar with this word and concept, but what exactly is communication skills? Why do we need it? How do we get better at it and how do we use it to influence people? Hold on to that thought for a minute while we discuss a more basic question.

"Are you good at communication?"

Go ahead and answer the question.

Qualities of good communication

Some of you would have answered, "Yes". The majority of you would have answered, "Well, you know, I am not exactly bad". Some of you would have answered a plain, "No". If you fall in the first category, then great. You are probably there already. If you are in the second category, it implies you are good and you are aware of the need for improvement. If you are in the third category, think again. Probably you are not as bad as you think. You are being too modest with yourself.

Let me rephrase the same question in two different ways.

Who according to you is a good communicator?
What exactly are the qualities of a good communicator?

Different people associate different qualities with good communication. Most people belive confidence, fluency of thoughts, proficiency in language and the attitude of the individual are the characteristics that make up a master communicator. Agreed. All these qualities enhance your communication skills.

In the end, it all boils down to one thing. "Are you able to convey your ideas to others without losing its essence?" We all have at least one friend who talks for hours but it would be impossible to understand anything. You all know that is not good communication. Talking is just one part of communication. Communication happens when the other person understands your point of view. I am sure almost all of us have this ability to convey what we think. Those of you who answered 'No' to the initial question and thought you were not good at communication, think again. If you can convey your thoughts clearly, you are probably not as bad a communicator as you think.

Communication Myths Busted

Effective communication is at the forefront of every business. A recent study revealed that many people receive confusing messages when they talk to people at work. Due to miscommunication, they end up doing the work twice, or worse inefficient work. When the top managers of an organization are unable to communicate clearly, it clearly implies there is still a lot of work to do regarding communication. There are a lot of myths surrounding communication. Let's bust them.

Myth 1 - English proficiency is a must for communication skills

This is the biggest myth among college students. English is the most widely used language in the world and all your interviews are going to be in English. Hence, having a good command over the English language is a very desirable skill. But linking proficiency in the language to communication skills is a big mistake. English is just a language, just like hundreds of other languages in the world. When we look at some of the greatest artists, poets, world leaders and politicians in the world, they do not even speak English. History has given us some of the greatest communicators who spoke languages like Greek, French, Spanish, Thamizh, Kannada, Telugu, Malayalam and Hindi. An Englishman can put all his efforts to learn Hindi, but he wouldn't be able to speak with the same ease as a person whose mother tongue is Hindi. So, don't worry if you are not able to match up with Shakespeare or Wordsworth. Don't bother if your grammar is not to the standards of Cambridge University. The most important thing is to convey your ideas in an efficient manner.

Myth 2 - Good talkers are good communicators

Well, there you have it. Good talkers are good talkers, end of story. Communication is a different ball game altogether. The loop of communication is complete only when the listener gives you feedback. It's the classic case of you narrating the entire story of the Mahabharata and the listener believes that Arjuna and Duryodhana are best friends. On the contrary, we have seen two people sail through life as best friends without even speaking a common language. Clearly, you don't have to be a great talker to express yourself.

Myth 3 - Communicating to impress is the best policy

There are two ways to communicate - communicate to express and communicate to impress. Putting in a deliberate effort to impress someone is not the right idea. You might come across as fake and desperate. Moreover, when we try to impress someone else, the very joy of communicating is lost. Think of the men in the stone age. They did not have any flowery language to impress people; they did not know fancy words to attract their mates. The only ever reason they communicated was to express themselves. In that kind of communication, there is a total expression of honesty and that is what people look forward to. Hence, communicating to express is always better than communicating to impress.

Myth 4 - Great communicators are born

Many people believe communication is a skill you are born with. Contrary to the belief, communication is not something you are born with; it is something you develop. It is not something you have; it is something you do. Communication skill is like a muscle in your body. The muscle doesn't develop by itself. The muscle doesn't develop by only watching motivational videos. A combination of the right diet and the right exercise routine is what helps you develop your muscles. In the same way, communication skill is a mental muscle that will develop by consistent practice. It is definitely not a one-day game. It is more like a test match which involves a lot of patience. Well, here is an interesting concept. If you practice the skills so well and you get so good at it, you start communicating with such ease, finesse and confidence. That is when people say, "Oh! He is a born communicator!"

Good negotiators are good communicators

If busting these myths was not good enough to make you believe you are not actually bad at communication, the following incidents from your own life will. Think of a time when you have been to the store to buy a pair of jeans. If the shopkeeper quotes a price which you know is much higher than the market price, would you buy it without questions? Say, you know the price of a particular brand of jeans is Rs 1500, but he quotes Rs 2000. You wouldn't pay just like that. You are sure to argue and also go on to let him know you have different options and that his store is not the only one in town. Eventually, you would have bought that pair of jeans for a much lower cost. Well done, you are a good negotiator.

If you have ever bargained to reduce the fare of an auto ride, well done. If you have convinced your parents to lend you pocket money to go on a weekend trip with friends, well done. If you have convinced your school teacher to give you an extra 2 marks for your answer, well done. If you have successfully convinced your friend to go and watch a movie he was reluctant to watch, well done. If you were ever late to class and convinced your professor to let you in, well done. If you have ever forgotten your wallet at home and still managed to buy that fried rice by convincing the restaurant guy you will pay later, well done.

More than once in your life, you have been successful at negotiation. Every day, life throws a lot of situations where you have to be good communicators to just survive. Now that you realize you have come out with flying colours on a lot of occasions, you know for sure you are not a bad communicator. The actual need is to fine-tune your skills so it gives you that winning edge in Personal Interviews and other formal settings.

It's all in the perspective

Long long ago, so long ago, there lived six wise men who claimed to know everything under the sun; well almost everything. None of them had seen an elephant in their lives.

They were blindfolded and made to touch an elephant so they could figure out what it looks like. The six men happened to touch different parts of the elephant and they put forward their opinions.

The first man touched the leg of the elephant. "Oh, the elephant looks like a tree", he proclaimed. The second man touched the tail of the elephant. "Oh, the elephant looks like a rope", he exclaimed. The third man touched the central part of the body of the elephant. "Oh, the elephant looks like a massive wall", he announced. The fourth man touched the tusk of the elephant. "Oh, the elephant looks like a spear", he thought aloud. The fifth man touched the trunk of the elephant. "Oh, the elephant looks like a snake", he declared. Finally, the sixth man touched the ears of the elephant. "Oh, the elephant looks like a leaf", he was confident.

The six men started to argue on who is right and who is wrong. What do you think? From their own perspective, everyone is right. Their knowledge is limited and they are speaking only from that angle. But, is anyone actually right? Absolutely not! The elephant looks like an elephant, doesn't it? It doesn't look like the leaf or the wall or the rope or the snake or the spear or the tree. This clearly illustrates it is extremely important to understand where the other person is coming from when communicating.

Let's get into the lives of three little boys from different parts of the world. Each of them is 5 years old. All three see an aeroplane flying. Let's quickly analyse how they react. The boy from America jumps in joy and tries to catch it. He aims high. Travelling in an aeroplane is not a big deal for him. He has already travelled multiple times in an aeroplane; he wants to catch it; in his mind, he owns the plane. The boy from India looks at the flight in awe. He can only dream of travelling in a plane, but every time he sees it, he feels good. The boy from a nation at war hides inside a bunker the moment he sees an aeroplane. He has had the most terrible experience of seeing bombs dropped from planes during the war. This story is a clear indicator that people react to the exact same events in extremely opposite ways depending on their previous experiences.

Let's look at a classic example. Look at the picture given below.

A Study of Perspectives

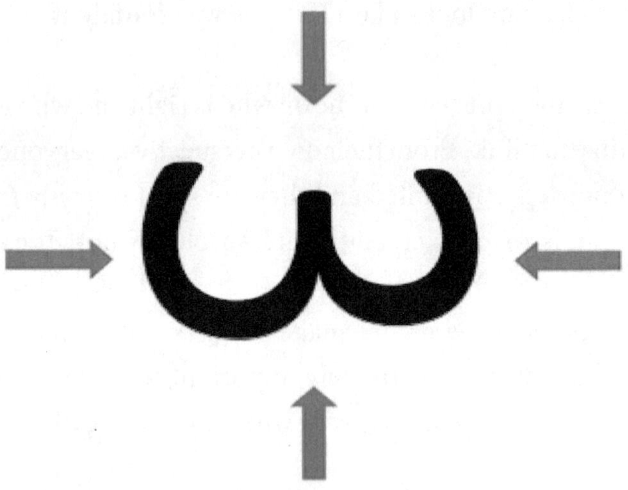

The same image conveys four different meanings depending on the position from where you look.

From the left, it is '3'.
From the right, it is 'E'.
From the top, it is 'M'.
From the bottom, it is 'W'.

When a simple image can look different depending on the angle from which you look, keep in mind that people have different experiences. It's only natural that everyone doesn't look at things, the exact same way.

Comm-You-Nication

There is a three-letter word which gets everyone's attention. It is one of the most commonly used words. The word is 'You'. We were all little kids once. At that time, all we thought of was, 'me, me and me!' We only thought of ourselves and how others would fit into our universe. We grew up, but that basic thinking hasn't changed much. Great communicators understand this. They always push the 'I' to the background and concentrate on the 'You'. Successful salespeople understand it the best. They never say, "This pen writes really well". They always say, "You are going to love this pen". They never say, "The LED TV has the best picture quality". They always say, "You and your family are going to have a fabulous experience watching movies on this TV". When you put the other person's interest first, you come across as the most wonderful person in his subconscious mind. Think of communication as a giant revolving spotlight. Make sure it shines less on you and most of the time, it shines on the person you are communicating with.

Components of Communication

Communication happens in different ways. We are all lucky to have the gift of structured languages now. Men and women who lived thousands of years ago didn't have that opportunity. Still, they found a way to express themselves. They used sign language. They understood different types of sounds and people in the forests knew the meaning of each sound. This helped them convey threats to fellow humans so they could prep themselves for what was coming. The 'whistle' is still recognised as an important method of communication by soldiers in the military. People who work with massive machinery are taught how to whistle so they could communicate with each other amidst heavy sounds.

If language is not even necessary to communicate, then how exactly does communication happen? Well, it is a mix of various elements combined together. But what conveys more and what conveys less? Let's look at what the best minds in the world think about this fascinating phenomenon. Experts have analysed this concept and arrived at the following conclusion.

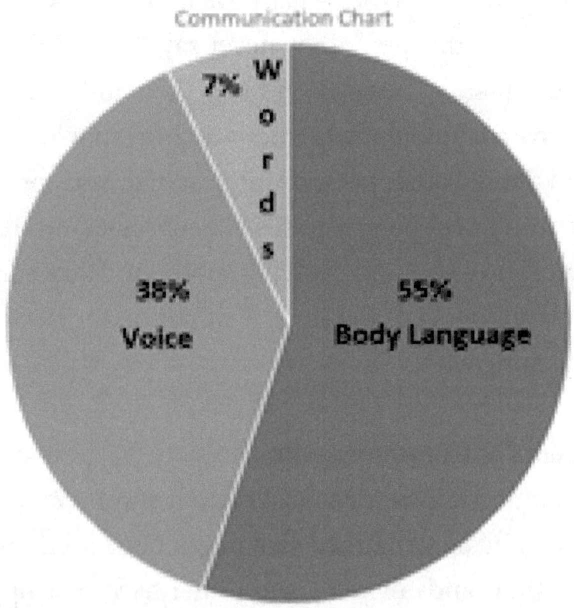

If you are surprised at the above chart, you are not alone. When I stumbled across the research for the first time, I was taken aback. I began to research further and was surprised to know there are other researches too which confirm these findings. Professor of psychology, Albert Mehrabian came to the exact same conclusion when he proposed his communication model as follows.

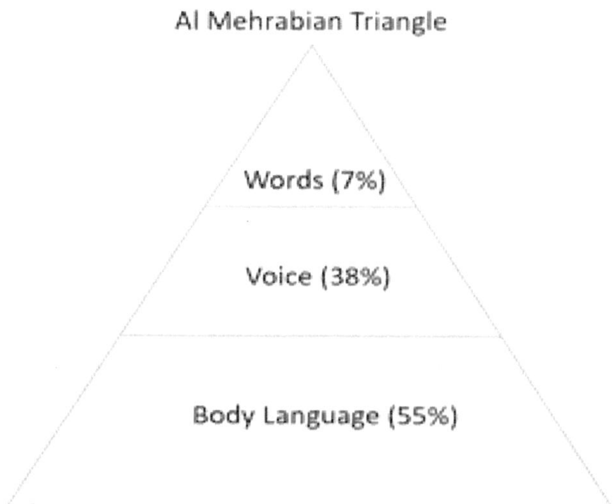

Both these studies confirm that a massive 55% of communication happens via Body Language. The Voice accounts for 38% while the Spoken Word has only 7% of the impact. Do remember this holds good only for face to face communication. In a telephonic conversation, the effect of voice takes precedence. If you are still not convinced about these findings, let's look at each of them in detail. The study of each of these components warrants an individual chapter for themselves. We will discuss body language and voice modulation in the next couple of chapters.

Now that we know the importance of communication, the qualities of good communication and the components that make it, let's get to the 'how'.

After all, knowledge is not power.
The application of knowledge is!

CHAPTER
Two
BODY LANGUAGE

Picture your lecturer walking into your classroom. He is visibly frustrated and looking furious. The very first words he utters are the customary, "I am extremely happy to see you!" Would you believe him? Would you even agree he might actually be happy? Absolutely not! The reason is simple. The lecturer's body is lying and it is not in congruence to his speech. Simply put, his actions are not matching his words. Hence, he loses his credibility and comes across as fake.

When I started doing theatre plays, I was always nervous about my lines. I was always worried I would forget my lines. I used to put so much emphasis on delivering the exact dialogues that my acting would go for a toss. After a particular rehearsal, my director informed me I was probably going to end up as a very bad actor. I was surprised at the comment because I had not forgotten even one single dialogue. I questioned him and he told me something very important that day. He noticed, "Karthick, your body is lying. Your body is not in sync with your dialogues. It's very obvious you have mugged up your lines. The lines are coming out alright, but they don't really mean anything since it lacks credibility."

How true was that! The audience is paying to watch a character come alive on stage. All he is interested in is the story of that character. He doesn't have to get the exact lines uttered out. He doesn't even know what the lines are. As long as he sees an honest character, he is going to relate to it and connect with the actor. That incident made me realize the body plays such a massive part in communication.

Exam Blues

Let's take a classic example which will hold good for ages to come. We have all given exams in life - we like it or not. I am sure every one of you can relate if I say we always have a night out before the exams. In fact, for most of us, that is the only day we get to prepare for our exams. It doesn't matter if we have 10 days of study holidays, the day before the exam is when we get that elusive energy to prepare. We get to the exam hall 10 minutes before the official start time.

Now comes the interesting part. How many of you have the habit of looking at your friends' reactions before entering into the exam hall? Yes, we all do. It's only human nature to compare ourselves with our peers at crucial junctures in our lives. A few minutes before a semester/board exam definitely qualifies as a crucial moment for most of us. Think about the different kinds of reactions you get to see from your friends.

One of your friends would be walking up and down the corridor at such high speed clearly indicating he is nervous. Another friend of yours would be sweating profusely and his heart would be racing at the rate of knots. Well, we all know he is absolutely nervous. We all have that friend who prays the Lord Almighty summoning divine intervention to make him pass the exam. It's a clear give away he is tensed. Amidst all this, I am sure you will find one of your friends waltz through the exam hall, just a pen in hand and face as calm as a Zen master. His attitude clearly indicates he is as cool as a cucumber. As the old joke goes, we can infer two different things from his body language. He has either prepared really well for the exam or absolutely nothing to a point he doesn't really care.

If these reactions are funny, what follows is even more fascinating. You are now inside the examination hall and comfortably seated. As soon as you receive your question paper, how many of you have the habit of looking at your friends' reactions? I am sure most of us do. One look at your friend's face will clearly tell you how he is going to fare in his exam. If he looks demoralized, you know he will struggle to just pass. Psychology suggests we always want our best friends to be in the same boat as us. So, without any doubt, you will glance in your best friend's direction. If he expresses the same emotion as you, then well and fine. But, if you feel the question paper is tough and your best friend's face shows happiness, you get worried. You actually start to wonder what's wrong and how on earth is he happy when you are clueless.

YOU CANNOT NOT COMMUNICATE

We have all experienced the above incidents in our lives. Now comes the crucial part. Think of all your friends you saw outside and inside the examination hall. Did they actually come and talk to you? Did they even utter a single word to you expressing their emotions? NO. You concluded one of them was nervous. You deciphered the others were tense, cool or happy. You, in fact, predicted their results just by looking at the way they moved and looked. In other words, they communicated with you without uttering a single word. They communicated with you even without realizing you are looking at them; that you even existed.

Yes, they communicated with you using their body language. In other words, you always communicate - you like it or not; you know it or not.

You Cannot Not Communicate

With the above illustrations, I am sure you will agree with the communication experts that more than half of our communication happens through body language.

Actions speak louder than words

All of a sudden, the proverb 'Actions speak louder than words' makes absolute sense, doesn't it? Let's look at one more example which happens in our everyday lives. Visualize yourself getting stuck in a new part of town. Your friend has invited you to a party at his home and you are trying to get there. You do not exactly know the location of his house, but you know it's right next to the Gandhi statue. Being the smooth communicator that you are, you stop by a popular bakery in that area and ask someone,

"Bro, how do I get to the Gandhi statue?"

"That's easy bro", bang comes the reply. "Take the straight road and at the junction, take the right", he finishes triumphantly with so much confidence.

Everything is perfect, except he stretched out his left hand while saying 'right'. Now, you are confused. He said 'right' but he so confidently gestured with his left hand. You are now left to crack the Da Vinci code. Which one would you trust?

Which is more likely to be correct?

Studies have confirmed someone is more likely to make a mistake in choosing the right word, but rarely does his body lie. So, you confirm with him again,

"Bro, are you sure it's right? You say right, but you are showing your left hand".

"Oh, sorry brother", he apologizes. *"I actually meant left"*, he signs off with that same confidence.

Your body doesn't usually lie. Even when you are trying to lie deliberately, your body will be a tell-tale sign to the experts you are not speaking the truth. Hence, body language is the most crucial part of communication. Let's see how we can use body language to project positivity, radiate energy and come across as a master communicator.

How to project the right body language?

Body language, by definition, is the type of non-verbal communication where physical actions are used to convey the information, instead of words. Starting with your head to toe, everything is part of your body and whatever you do with them to communicate is considered body language. Body Language is a major study in itself and tons of books have been written on the topic. The scope of this book is to visit the basics which will help you in your day to day communication and interviews. It will also provide you with the basics for business communications.

You might wonder you have been getting along fine all these years and what is the sudden need to analyse body language as a subject now? The answer is simple. It is more important now than ever because you are not considered a kid anymore. That tag was left behind at school. College life is your official entry into adult life and from now on, everything you do is scrutinized. You don't get a leeway anywhere citing the 'kids' card. It's extremely critical you do not convey the wrong information accidentally through body language blunders. The last thing you want is to make a body language blunder and not even realize it. In this book, let's discuss the most important ones. Most of them are fairly simple and quite obvious, but then beauty lies in simplicity. Success doesn't happen by chance. It happens by doing the little things right, every single time.

Eye Contact

Eye contact, by definition, is the state in which two individuals are looking directly into each other's eyes. It's not exactly rocket science to realize that looking into the eyes of the person with whom we are talking to (or the lack of it) conveys a lot of things. The study of eye contact is also how and how much do we look into the other person's eyes while communicating with him. I am fortunate to have the experience of thousands of hours as a soft skills trainer in college classrooms. It is a lesson in eye contact by itself.

When I am in a classroom session, I just have to look at a student's eyes to figure out how he is feeling. If he is looking away from me whenever I try to make eye contact with him, I know he doesn't understand anything because he is simply not interested. When a student is looking at his watch very often instead of looking into my eyes, it is very obvious he is really bored and waiting for the class to get over. On the positive side, if he is directly looking into my eyes, I know for a fact he is actually listening and probably enjoying my class. That is the most honest feedback I could ever get. All those official forms the students or audience fill up at the end of the session may not really convey the truth. One look at their eyes and I will know whether they really enjoyed the session or not.

What do you think? Is it good to have good eye contact? Common sense suggests YES. Eye contact conveys confidence. It definitely provides that connect, but as always too much of anything is good for nothing. Eye contact is pleasant, but that doesn't mean we should be looking into the other person's eyes 100% of the time. Staring is never good and most of the time, it comes across as creepy.

As a general rule, in any formal setting (when you are talking to your professor, your HOD or your interviewer), it is good to have 75% to 80% of eye contact with whom you are communicating. It's okay to have close to 100% eye contact while listening. While talking, look into the other person's eyes but break away once in a while. This rule holds good for all professional communication.

The rule of eye contact is different for personal interactions though. Different people exhibit different levels of eye contact depending on the comfort level they share with each other. For example, a husband would have very intimate eye contact with his wife. A mother would have much intimate eye contact with her baby. In fact, different cultures perceive eye contact in different ways. The Western world encourages eye contact professionally while the Eastern cultures reserve intimate eye contact only for their personal interactions.

Apart from confidence, eye contact conveys honesty. Good eye contact implies you are telling the truth. It conveys you are speaking without trying to make things up. Investigation officers look for eye contact clues during the interrogation process to pin down suspects. It's generally considered when a person is lying, guilty or embarrassed, he avoids eye contact.

Think of a college student trying to tell his dad he has flunked 4 subjects in the semester. Do you think he would be able to directly look into his eyes and say, "Hey Dad, I flunked!" Well, it is possible, but the chances are pretty slim. More likely, he is going to look down and probably say something like,

"Dad...er... Hey Dad... the results came today and er...."

Eye contact is a beautiful game in the professional arena. The men and women who understand the rules and play it to perfection are more likely to be successful. Poets have declared eye contact to be dangerous, but a lovely thing. Psychologists have announced eye contact is more powerful than words will ever be.

Drama writers have opined eye contact is how souls catch fire. In short, eye contact hits you like a bullet. Take the right aim and in the game of communication, you are sure to hit the target.

Facial Expressions

Researchers say the human face is capable of displaying 7000 different expressions. Yes, you read the number right. For some of us who think, 'happy and sad' are the only two emotions our face can express, this would come as a total surprise.

Face is the index of the mind

We are all familiar with the idea our face tells a million stories that no words ever will. When you go back home from your college in the evening, you don't really have to tell your mother how your day went. Merely by looking at your face, she can tell your exam results. She can precisely guess how your project review went. Face is the embodiment of our state of mind. Here are a few states of mind that our face is capable of expressing.

➢ Happy
➢ Sad
➢ Embarrassed
➢ Guilty
➢ Excited
➢ Worried
➢ Calm
➢ Terrified
➢ Nervous
➢ Relaxed

➤ Thankful

➤ Content

During the 2016 T20 World Cup match between India and Australia, I realized something invaluable. I was out on an important assignment and when I came back home, the match was already halfway through. I switched on the TV eager to check the score; excited to know how India was doing. As it turned out, I didn't even have to look at the scorecard. All I had to do was look at Virat Kohli's face and I clearly knew the state of the match. The range of expressions he showed was simply amazing. India was initially struggling and I could see his face looked tense, but determined. As the match progressed and as India began to take control, his face was more relaxed and calmer. As India finally crossed the line during a tense chase, his face expressed a sense of triumph and relief. What better way to understand the importance of facial expressions!

During the final year of my college, I stayed in the hostel. My roommate was a huge fan of the American Television Sitcom 'F.R.I.E.N.D.S'. He used to stay up all night and binge-watch the episodes. I was an early sleeper. Intending not to disturb me, he would put his headphones on and watch the show on the computer. There were days when I was unable to sleep and I used to look at the screen from my bed. It was fascinating. When the sound is cut off, it's amazing how many different facial expressions you notice. I watched one entire episode without sound and to my surprise, I was clearly able to understand what was happening. Good actors don't really need lines to express their emotions. Their faces are enough. If our facial expressions can convey so much, how do we use them to generate positivity? How do we radiate energy? Well, the simplest weapon of them all is right there with us. It is just 2 inches below our eyes. I am talking about the 'smile'.

Smile

I was never a very bright student in Physics, but I was very clear about one thing.

Energy can neither be created nor destroyed

Yes, a simple smile radiates energy. I was once walking in my office corridor with a million thoughts in my mind. I was stressed, thinking of the bills to pay, phone calls to make and deadlines to meet. Suddenly, a stranger walked past me and all he gave me was a 'smile'. Well, that was enough. It put a smile on my face too. In fact, I should say, it put the smile back on my face. Suddenly all my problems appeared trivial and it helped me resolve each one of them with ease. Ah! The Power of the Smile.

Smile is a small curve that straightens many things

The law of Physics continues to state,

It can only be transformed from one form to another,
in an equivalent amount

So, smiling is a great way of spreading positive energy across the room. A smiling person comes across as happy, positive and easily approachable. These are exactly the skills you require to win friends. However, the game is simple, but not easy. It is just not about widening the lips two inches on either side. People are much smarter today to understand the difference between a genuine smile and a fake one. Well, after all these years, let's learn to smile.

The Winning Smile

Communication experts have always advised us, for the smile to be genuine, it has to come from the heart. Well, in most cases, we see people for the very first time and it is very difficult to smile from the heart. A smile filled with sarcasm is considered arrogant. A smile that is not sincere doesn't really give a good impression. It comes across as very artificial. If you smile at someone immediately on seeing them, it is likely you would come across as over-anxious or worse, desperate. Folks in the HR department, who are most likely to interview you are trained to catch those little glitches in our body language.

During my second year in college, we had invited one of the film celebrities to be the chief guest of our annual cultural event. I was a big fan of her and somehow got into the line of boys who would be receiving her when she got down from her car. As soon as she got down from her car, I smiled at her and can you believe it, she smiled back! She smiled back immediately. I was over the moon. I couldn't really explain my feelings. Here is a celebrity who I have adored all these years. Now, she is right in front of me, in flesh and blood, and smiling at me. I was flying. I was in cloud nine.

Well, it didn't take long for my excitement to come crashing down. Life is a great leveller, isn't it? If you see the incredible highs, you are sure to see the lows soon. The celebrity walked past me and gave the exact same smile to every single person in the line. It was not exclusive to me. I didn't feel special anymore.

Big winners do not smile immediately. They always take an extra second for themselves. But that one second is crucial. After that, they give a big beaming smile which spreads slowly. Just like the early morning rays from the sun, the slow spreading, big beamer makes the recipient feel good. It has got a personalized touch and puts you across as someone who is considerate, but not desperate.

Gestures

Gestures are any hand or head movements we use to express an idea or thought. They are used either in conjunction with speech or instead of speech. Long before the languages of the world took shape, people used a lot of gestures while communicating. Those gestures are so influential they can tell you the power equation between the people involved. Even if you don't hear a single word of communication between two people, you know who is the boss just by looking at their gestures.

We use gestures while talking and listening. Let's look at a situation which most of us would have encountered. Picture yourself having just won a badminton tournament. You are excited. Your best friend who is walking towards you at a distance of 50 meters gestures to you to enquire about the result. How will you convey you have won? When you are conveying your victory, your hands automatically go up, don't they? It would be impossible for any human to convey his victory by pushing his hands in the downward direction. Similarly, if you are trying to convey you have lost your purse or lost the match, your hands automatically go down. It's only human nature that your body aligns itself with your speech and thoughts. That's precisely why gestures are extremely important in conveying your state of mind.

Have you ever listened to politicians speak? They gesture a lot with their hands. They make sure they have a very open body language. Have you ever wondered why every single politician in the world follows the same technique? Is it a mere coincidence? Of course not. Politicians are taught to speak that way on stage. Generally, they speak in front of a large audience. There might be hundreds or even thousands of people. Do you think the audience member sitting in the very last row will actually listen to every word he says? It is likely he has come for the free meal they have promised at the end of the speech.

The physical distance between the speaker and the listener is a huge factor. This is why every politician makes expansive gestures while delivering his speech. He provides a visual treat to the audience with his gestures. On seeing this, the person in the last row gets motivated even if he doesn't exactly listen to the speech. He believes his leader is onto something. I recommend you watch how politicians use gestures to make an impact. The great leaders of the world use gestures to plant ideas in their listeners' subconscious minds. American president-elect candidates practise their gestures multiple times before getting into political debates to get that winning edge against their opponent.

I have had the fortune of acting in a lot of theatre plays. I love the stage and sometimes I get a chance to act in front of the camera as well. Here is the interesting part. Performing for the exact same scene in front of the camera is totally different to the stage. In front of the camera, you are expected to be subtle. A small smile can express a million emotions. In front of a live audience on stage, my director always advises me to use expansive gestures. The audience member sitting 25 rows from the stage will not be able to appreciate subtlety in acting. He needs to see those massive movements and expansive gestures to get impressed by the actor. That's precisely why a lot of movie buffs perceive play actors to be overacting. But now, you know why we do it.

In a similar vein, our head can gesture a lot while communicating. We all use the 'head nod' to indicate 'yes'. Shaking the head from side to side conveys 'no' around the world. A slight nod of the head can be used to greet someone. Some people gesture their head downwards to mean, 'come here'. The head nod can also be used to indicate you have understood something while listening.

In short, gestures either replace your words or reiterate what you say. It gives additional power to your words. When your mom asks you to come home before 9 PM, she is just saying it. But if she accompanies those words with a gesture of the index finger pointing at you, you know she really means it. You better be home by 8:59 PM latest.

Gestures mean different in different countries

Any study on gestures is not complete without understanding the gestures you can use and most importantly, the ones you cannot use in certain countries. A gesture which is very commonly used and perfectly normal in India might be seen as a rude gesture in Thailand. A slang that is very common in the USA might offend the British. Just like table manners, gestures also mean different things in different cultures. When you are visiting a new country, you will surely make an effort to learn a few words of the local language. However, it is more important to learn the gestures that should not be used in that country. The last thing you want is to unintentionally offend a local and get into trouble.

The 'thumbs-up' sign which we use to say, "All the best" or "Win" or "Done" is seen as an insulting gesture in Iraq and Afghanistan. The 'backwards peace' sigh which we so commonly use here is considered an insult in the United Kingdom. The OK sign is considered rude in Brazil and the list goes on.

So, the use of gestures is a vital part of your body language. Let it flow naturally. Don't overdo it. You don't have to be a Shah Rukh Khan every time you talk to someone. At the same time, don't practice closed gestures with your hands. The moment you fold your hands, your mind doesn't feel that open anymore. On the positive side, wide-open arms make you feel abundance and you become more welcoming to new ideas. The more open your gestures are, the more confident you feel. You come across as more confident and the way people react to you will change for the better if you master the art of using gestures.

Handshakes
Every business interaction (including interviews) begins and ends with a handshake. How important do you think are

handshakes? Fasten your seat belts as you prepare yourself for the news. A handshake can actually make or break your interview. It can make or break a million-dollar deal. A handshake can actually make you feel good or bad. Let's quickly discuss the different kinds of handshakes.

A handshake without showing any kind of interest in the meeting is called the 'dead fish handshake'. Needless to say, people with dead fish handshakes create a terrible first impression. Their chances of getting through the interview are remote. If you only offer the fingers, it conveys your diffidence. Never offer just the fingers. People who get their palm high up and place it over the palm of the other person are said to have the 'Topper' handshake. They come across as aggressive and in today's world, being aggressive is not a winning trait. The opposite of the 'dead fish' handshake is the 'Bone Crusher'. They shake the hands so hard you might have to take an X-ray after the handshake. They come across as arrogant. Do not give bone crushers as we wouldn't want to be on the receiving end ourselves. If these handshakes are not recommended, what is a good handshake?

The All-American Handshake

The best and the universally recommended way to shake hands in any professional scenario (including interviews) is called the All-American handshake. It has got the following characteristics.

➤ Hold the palm of the other person; not the wrist or the fingers.

➤ It should be firm, but not bone-crushing.

➤ Your hand is neither on top nor at the bottom of the other person's hand. It is at the same level, conveying equality.

➤ It should not be for more than 2 seconds.

- There should be one pump from the elbow (If the pump happens from the shoulders, it means you have overstretched your hand. If it happens from your wrist, you have not extended your hand enough.)
- Maintain a pleasant eye contact and smile while shaking hands.
- Do not shake hands if your palms are wet or sweaty. When someone offers a handshake when your palms are sweaty, just smile and let them know that your hands are sweaty and start a pleasant conversation.

A word of caution

If I was writing this book 6 months before, I would have asked you to offer handshakes whenever you meet someone in a professional setting. But the COVID-19 pandemic has changed the dynamics. All over the world, people have been advised not to shake hands and maintain social distancing. Hence, take a good judgement call. In these unprecedented times, it is perfectly understandable if you or the other person doesn't want to shake hands. I sincerely hope the pandemic ends soon and we return to the good old days of handshakes!

Fidgeting

Fidgeting is making small, unnecessary movements with your hands and feet. Tapping on the desk while talking, tapping the feet on the ground and adjusting your hair once too often are classic examples of fidgeting. It conveys nervousness and impatience. If you are able to hold yourself still, it conveys a strong personality. Fidgeting also diverts the attention of the listener. If you fidget while you talk, the listener doesn't know whether to concentrate on your words or to look at your fidgeting. The rule is simple

- avoid fidgeting if you want to come across as a powerful and confident personality.

Shoulders

We use the shoulders to convey a few things. Universally, the shoulder shrug means the person doesn't know or doesn't understand. If you want to know the energy and enthusiasm and the current state of mind of a person, just have a look at his shoulders. I was watching a football match between two great European clubs. Unfortunately, it turned out to be a one-sided affair. With only 30 seconds remaining on the clock for the final whistle, the score line read 4-1.

I was able to notice one striking difference between the body language of the two teams. The team that was trailing had given up all hope. Their energy levels were low and it was understandable because they virtually had no chance of winning. Their shoulders were slumped; they were drooping and it was a clear indicator they were waiting for the ordeal to end. On the other hand, the players from the winning team had their shoulders back as if to say, "Bring it on!" This is one body language you will notice with the CEOs and all the big shots. They never let their shoulders slump. Slumping the shoulders is a sign of defeat. So, get that shoulders tucked back and you will radiate confidence.

The Walk

Walking is a physical activity and hence it could be a direct reflection of your state of mind. A confident man is sure-footed, he doesn't look down while walking and always looks straight. I was always fascinated with how our walk can impact our energy levels. When I worked for an IT company, I used to take the morning bus to the office. Understandably, it was an early start to the day. We used to board the bus at 6:30 AM and by the time the bus reached the office at 7:45 AM, most of us would be pretty tired. The way every person gets down and walks to his cubicle is a very interesting study. People who love their work feel enthused about the day coming up. They get down and walk with absolute confidence. On the other hand, people who are terrified of their work walk as if they are being dragged by someone. One trick I have learnt over the years is to place my steps in a particular way.

Heel First, Toe Next

I always take medium-sized steps putting my heel down first followed by the toe. This is a proven method to get a spring in your step. You will sense the confidence and it helps you immensely before crucial moments in your life. Try this when you enter your interview room. Try this when you walk in for your group discussions. The difference a small tweak in your walking style can make is immense.

Sitting Posture

Remember the good old days in school? Every time, we leaned back to get too comfortable or leaned forward to lie down on our desks, our teachers kept saying one thing - "Sit Erect!" It still holds good even today. Leaning forward a little while listening shows interest. Leaning too far forward conveys you are uncomfortable. Never lean back too much while sitting in those recliner chairs. That gives an impression you are not attentive. Sit erect. Make yourself comfortable. Make sure your legs are not crossed at the ankles. Find a comfortable posture that relaxes you and at the same time makes you attentive.

Fake it till you make it

Body language is a huge study in itself and even a 1000-page book will not suffice to cover all its elements. However, we have covered the basics which will help you immensely in all formal communications. We all know the mind directly influences the body. But the most exciting thing to note is that the converse is also true. The body influences your mind immensely. Whenever you feel low, take a walk in the park. Go for a little jog. Shout aloud and dance your heart out. You will feel an adrenaline rush in your body and that will definitely cheer you up. Great motivational speakers do push-ups before they get on stage. This helps them create the energy they could transfer to their audience. Physical actions go a long way in making you feel better and energized.

Revisit these basics. Improving your body language doesn't happen overnight. It takes practice to get to a point where it feels natural. As is the case in any learning, there are four different stages. It's similar to the process of learning to ride a bike with gear. The first stage is called, '*Unconscious Incompetence*'. You do not know there is something called a bike and quite naturally, you don't know how to ride it. Then, you start to learn. You struggle with changing the gears. You struggle with balance. This stage is called '*Conscious Incompetence*'. You know there is a bike and you are aware you ought to learn a lot of things. Then, you get better at it. You learn how to balance. Every time, you change your gear, you concentrate a lot, but you are getting there. This stage is called '*Conscious Competence*'. The final stage is where you have become a really good rider. You are not conscious about the change of gears any more. It becomes second nature to you. You get on the bike and even without realizing what you do, you reach home. This stage is called, 'Unconscious Competence'.

This is exactly how a baby learns to walk. At first, she doesn't have the skill. Then, she struggles. Slowly, she gets the idea and finally, she walks without even giving a thought to it. Body Language is just like that. You might feel a little silly practising these things in the beginning. People might mock you. Well, there will always be people to mock you whenever you take a step in the right direction. Keep at it. A few months of practice and you don't have to worry about the basics any more. Experts don't do very difficult things. They always get the basics right. This is true in arts, sports and the business world.

Fake it till you make it

CHAPTER THREE
VOICE

Voice is the sound uttered through the mouth of living creatures, especially human beings. We humans associate emotions with voice. If you are feeling confident, you speak in a very assertive tone. A scared person speaks in a submissive tone and usually, it results in a very frail voice. An angry person tends to speak in an aggressive tone. Voice is a crystal-clear reflection of our state of mind, just like body language. If communication happens over the telephone, it takes even more importance. Over the telephone, the impact of voice is not 38%. It is close to 75% while the words account for the other 25%.

Your close ones will definitely find your state of mind with a small sample of your voice. I had a really tough day once and wanted to share it with my best friend. I called him and said, "Hello". There was a deafening silence on the line. After a few seconds, I mustered up all the courage to say, "Hello" again.

"Hey Karthick, are you alright?", bang came the response.
"I am!", I muttered weakly.
"No, you are not!", he was absolutely sure.

It's in the voice, ladies and gentlemen. One hello is enough for people close to you to find out your state of mind.

Leaders around the world have influenced elections with their great speeches. Winston Churchill, Nelson Mandela, Barack Obama and all great visionaries used voice as a potent weapon to define the course of their respective nations. Great presenters use their voice to wake up a sleeping audience. Parents use the power of voice to make their babies sleep. Almost all the great actors are known for their skill to modulate their voice while delivering punch lines. Needless to say, singers completely rely on their voice to record their best-selling albums. The right kind of voice modulation helps you connect easily with your communication partner.

Different people, different moods, different tone

You are naturally good at using different tones of voice. You use a different tone while speaking with your HOD as opposed to speaking with your friend. You don't speak with a baby and a teenager in the same tone. The tone of voice shows your intelligence in communication as well. If you are talking with a person who has just won the tennis tournament final, your voice is upbeat. If he had lost the final, your voice would be mellow. Your voice is a clear indicator of your mood and the environment.

Think of your favourite Radio Jockeys (RJs). They are the masters of voice modulation. They set the mood for their listeners and set the tone for the entire show with just the opening greeting. The RJ of the 7 AM show would scream out a "Goooood Morning Bengaluruuuuuuu". There is energy in the voice for the listeners to shake off their morning blues. The voice energizes the listeners and gets them out of bed. An afternoon show will have a more neutral tone of voice. That is intended for people who have just finished their lunch and wanting to have a quiet time. If the show is late at night, then the tone is usually mellow. It is very soothing so that the listeners feel good before getting to bed. It's very critical to ensure your voice projects confidence and hits the right chord.

People who watch sports on TV will definitely understand the importance of voice in communication. Sport without commentary is like food without salt. The commentator is communicating with you through his voice. Most of the time, you don't even get to see his face. Still, he is the voice who brings you the emotions of the match. Every Indian would remember Ravi Shastri's comment when Dhoni hit that six to win the 2011 Cricket World Cup Final.

Dhoni finishes off in style. A magnificent strike into the crowd! India lift the **World Cup** after 28 years!", Ravi Shastri exclaimed.

As much as we remember the match, as much as we remember that six, we all remember Ravi Shastri's commentary. The voice modulation was excellent. The highs and the lows of the voice is what makes commentary interesting. Football commentators do it the best. Football is a game where there is action every single minute. The tone of the commentary is always energetic, yet in defining moments, like when a goal is scored or when a penalty is awarded, the tone of voice gets even more energetic.

"Goaaaaalllllllllllll!!!!!!!!", the commentator would announce. If you had fallen asleep watching one of those Premier League matches late at night, you are sure to wake up listening to the commentary. How do some communicators have a great voice? How do they manage to enthral an audience? Let's look at a few characteristics of the voice.

Components of Voice

Volume

Volume is the sound of your voice. If you are angry, you tend to shout (high volume). If you are calm and relaxed, your volume is soft. If your team has scored a goal, you scream. If you intend to tell a secret, you whisper. If you want urgent help, you scream. In communication, the volume is very important. As the above examples show, the volume of your voice is representative of your emotions. During formal communication, it is very important to strike the right volume.

During my early days in theatre, I always struggled to find the right volume to deliver my lines. After one of my shows, my friend who was in the audience gave me feedback that my voice was too low. He had to struggle so much to hear me that he got a headache. In my next play, I overcompensated. I raised my volume so high that most of the audience got ear pain. "Who was that guy shouting all the time?", was the only feedback I got and my acting was completely ignored. Hence, it's very important to find the right volume when you are talking. Don't be too loud or too low. Similar to finding that perfect volume in your TV, adjust your volume so it is pleasant to the listener. More importantly, keep it at a level that is comfortable for you. Don't strain your vocal cords too much while speaking.

Pace

Pace is the speed at which you talk. If you are nervous or scared, you tend to speak very fast. If you are trying to explain an abnormal event and if you believe you are in danger at that moment, your rate of speech goes very high. If you are calm and relaxed, your rate of speech is much lower. The important factor to note here is the WPM (Words Per Minute). Most people speak at a speed of 4 to 5 syllables per second. Given that most words in English have 2 to 3 syllables, the average English speaker talks at 120 to 130 WPM. However, it is possible radio presenters and voice over artists speak at a slightly higher rate - around 160 WPM. They do it to keep their speech exciting and also to impart more information in the prescribed time limit.

You must have come across professors who either speak too fast or too slow. Listening to someone who speaks too fast can be difficult to keep up with. You need to stress yourself to follow what he is talking and chances are you will soon give up. On the other hand, speaking too slow is a sure-fire way of boring the other person. So, find the right pace for yourself. Record your voice for a minute by reading a paragraph into your phone's voice recorder. Count the number of words. If it falls between 120 and 130, you are good.

Pause

Pause refers to the breaks we take in sentences. We usually pause at the end of a thought. We also pause when we say something important so that we give time for the information to sink in. Great speakers pause for dramatic effect. CEOs use it to great effect during their product launches. It gives the audience that extra second for the message to sink in. Our brain gets a great sense of satisfaction if we ourselves figure out something as opposed to everything being spoon-fed. For this very reason, it is very important to pause while communicating.

Tone

Tone of voice is the attitude that the speaker projects. When you are talking with a friend, the tone is casual. When you are talking with your professor on a regular day, it is semi-formal. But when you are talking with your principal to get permission for an inter-college cultural competition, the tone is formal. When you are talking in an interview or a group discussion, the tone has to be formal. SMS and WhatsApp culture have given us a lot of acronyms for regularly used words. 'LOL', we say for 'Laughing Out Loud'. 'TYSM', we say for 'Thank You So Much'. The culture has influenced us so much that we use abbreviations even while talking. There are a lot of slang words which can pass off with a friend but not with your college Principal or interviewer. Great communicators always align their tone of voice with the people they are with and the situation they are in.

Stress

Stress is the emphasis you use on a certain word or a certain syllable in a word. Depending on which word is stressed, the meaning of the sentence can change totally.

People from different countries speak English in a slightly different way. While speaking the same word, they stress different syllables giving way to different accents. That's why we often hear people say they understand the British accent but not the

American accent and vice versa. The stress on the syllables of the words is essential to get the right pronunciation of words leading to clarity in voice.

I have had the good fortune of working in Yorkshire, England for a few months during my IT career. I loved every bit of the place and had some great experiences. However, getting an Englishman to pronounce my name right was a tough challenge. The cab driver called me "Caddick". The gas agency addressed me as "Kardick". My customers at the office always called me "Kathik". Different accents in a language are like different flavours in ice creams - each unique but nice in its own way. I recommend stressing important words when you communicate. This helps you put across your point in an emphatic way.

Pitch and Intonation

Pitch refers to the rise and fall of our voice when we speak. It's the highs and the lows that make life interesting. In a similar way, it's the ups and downs that keep your talk interesting. Too much of anything is good for nothing. If you speak in a monotone for a considerable length of time, your conversation comes across as bland. Don't blame the other person if he falls asleep in no time listening to your monotone. Even in an ECG, a blank line indicates the heart has stopped beating. If you want your communication to feel lively, ensure to punctuate it with highs and lows. The graph of your voice must be like a wave. This keeps the others interested and most importantly, awake. As they say,

If the audience is sleeping,
somebody should wake up the speaker

The change in tone that created Bahubali

I believe most of you are familiar with the movie 'Bahubali'. It is one of the biggest box office hits of the century. We all wonder at the magnificence of the movie and the amount of effort the director must have put in to realize his magnum opus. You might think the seeds for the movie must have been sown at least 2 years before the shoot. But director Rajamouli says, it was much before that.

Rajamouli's first opportunity as a director is the one he got to direct an ad film for the Govt of Andhra Pradesh. It is his first day as a lead director and he is understandably very nervous about the entire process. He is literally shivering from head to toe. His body language clearly shows a man who is not in control. The man who gave Rajamouli the opportunity, Mr Mukherjee walks into the sets at that point. He wants to have a check on how the shoot is going. Rajamouli begins to tremble. If Mr Mukherjee sees the director terrified, there is every chance that Rajamouli's career is done and dusted. In another 60 seconds, Mukherjee will be inside the set.

What does the director do?

Rajamouli raises his voice. He begins to shout at the crew. He gives instructions to the artists, the light boys and the rest of the crew. Some of it is right, while the others are wrong, but it doesn't matter. Mukherjee sees that Rajamouli is a confident man and he is handling things pretty well. He gives a pat on Rajamouli's back and says, "Good job!" Remember, not even a single scene had been shot till now. He walks off happily and Rajamouli lives to fight another day. He starts to feel good about the whole thing now. He feels more confident. Remember, just 60 seconds ago, he was freezing.

The beauty of this incident doesn't end here. Rajamouli's change of tone has a sudden impact on the rest of the crew too. His voice sounds so confident that the artists, the light boys and the makeup team start listening to him as if every single word he says is gospel. They start to believe, 'Here is a director with whom I can't mess with'. His ad film turns out to be great and as they say, the rest is history.

Rajamouli goes on to become one of the greatest and most successful directors in Indian cinema. To think of it now that all this happened because of a small change in voice modulation is incredible, isn't it?

The human voice is a very powerful instrument in communication. The great heroes of the world became one by raising their voices at the right time. Use your voice, quite literally to become a hero in communication.

"Words mean more than what is set down on paper. It takes the human voice to infuse them with deeper meaning"

–Maya Angelou

CHAPTER Four
LISTENING SKILLS

How many people do we need for communication to happen? Communication can be of two types - 'one to one' or 'one to many'. Some would argue there is a third type of communication in which a person talks to himself. Well, we all do it sometimes. When I am trying to complete that fourth set of squats in the gym; when the body starts to give up, I find my inner motivational voice - "Come on Karthick, you can do it", it would scream. People who meditate, love their quiet time and communicate with their inner self. But communicating with self to find a deeper meaning of life is a vast topic. It is for another day and for another book. In a regular sense, we need at least two people for communication to happen. There is the talker and most importantly, the listener.

Communication, by definition, is the transfer of thoughts or ideas or opinion from one person to another. Hence, without an active listener, talking becomes a useless exercise. Effective listening is the ability to understand the speaker. It should be used to provide feedback to the speaker so that he knows his message is getting conveyed.

The difficult part of communication

You have been used to sitting in a classroom setting for more than 12 years now. You are the best bet to answer the following question correctly.

"Which is the more difficult skill? Talking or Listening?"

I can literally hear you scream out your lungs and say that listening is more difficult. Well, in my opinion, you are bang on. You are 100% right. When I talk, I say something which I already know. If I am expressing my own thoughts, it's not really difficult because I already have an interest attached to it. But listening is a different ball game altogether. You will hear what the other person says, no doubt. But then, do you really understand him? Unless you are listening effectively, it is a big NO. Let's see the factors that make the process of listening so difficult.

Listening Challenges

The listening capacity of the mind

The most important culprit is science itself. We discussed the average human being can talk at 120 to 130 WPM. But the listening capacity of the mind is much more. We can actually listen at 400-450 words per minute (if anyone is able to talk at that rate). Hence, only one-fourth capacity of the mind is actually getting used while listening. The mind is free the rest of the time and it doesn't really know what to do. Our minds wander and get distracted. Primarily, there are two kinds of distractions.

Physical distractions

Recently, I was taking a session on 'Tips to crack Personal Interviews' for final year students. The session was going absolutely great. The students were really attentive and I was enjoying the session. I was learning a lot from them as well. Just as I was making an extremely important point, "knock-knock", somebody was at the door. Suddenly, nobody cared about career-defining learning anymore. Everyone including me was looking at the door. It's only human that our brain reacts immediately to anything that breaks the pattern. A knock on the door and someone walking in breaks the current pattern and it takes some time for our minds to get the focus back on. Another day, in the middle of a group discussion class, it started raining. The participants started to talk about the rain instead of the topic given. A loud sound, the smell of rain, a friend from another department peeping through the window etc are all physical distractions. It takes special focus to not get distracted.

I have had the privilege of conducting hundreds of team-building activities for corporate organizations. Employees bond together and have a great time. They get an unforgettable experience. Most of the days, I do a pretty good job at it and my clients get super excited. On the contrary, I remember one day when things fell apart. The participants were in the middle of an exciting activity when the client decided to open the lunch counter. The smell of biryani is something which is hard to resist for most of us. Within a few seconds, all the energy and enthusiasm I had built with the activity went up in smoke. Once the food counter was opened, I could see the participants leaving midway through the activity to grab those chicken nuggets. This is another form of physical distraction. After all, you need to be a special kind of genius to compete against food… and win.

Mental distractions

I was once handling a session on 'Presentation Skills' for a bunch of very enthusiastic students. It was my fourth session with the class. The entire class had been really attentive for the previous three sessions. On that day though, I could sense something was different. None of them was listening to me. They were discussing among themselves and worse, checking their mobile phones. I started to wonder if something was wrong with me. I thought, probably I was wearing a torn shirt or there was grease on my face. Luckily, the mystery did not last long. One of them broke the ice and let me know they were awaiting their semester exam results any minute and that's why they have been checking their mobile phones. Well, that explains it.

If you are on the road and find out your wallet is missing, you will not be able to concentrate on anything else until you figure out where it is. If Virat Kohli is batting on 99, cricket buffs will not be able to listen to the class, until they know he has scored his century. If your favourite star's movie has just been released in the cinemas, your mind is on the reviews from the First Day First Show and not on the lecture. Apart from this, there are a million things running in our minds all the time which directly impacts our listening abilities.

Uninterested in the topic

I am a big fan of movies and cricket. If I get the right conversation partner and our frequencies match, I can talk on those topics for hours together. It is also possible if I keep talking cricket passionately to someone who doesn't really enjoy the game, I am going to bore him. We watch movies which are three hours long. If we are interested, we can listen for a long time. However, if the topic is boring for us, we wouldn't be able to listen even for a short period of time.

Difference of opinion

Our thoughts travel in a particular direction. Our brains are wired in a particular way, depending on the beliefs that we already have. If we hear an opinion that is contrary to our existing one, there is a good chance our mind gets tuned out while listening to it. If you have seen political debates on TV recently, you will surely agree with two things. You will see a lot of people talking and hear a lot of noise.

Chances of the viewers getting a headache - 100%
Chances of any meaningful communication - Zero

I am a big fan of Mahendra Singh Dhoni. I love it when I am discussing the positives about him. But if someone is criticizing him (a different opinion from mine), I find it very difficult to listen. I can hear, but I don't really listen. My mind seems to develop some kind of a filter which lets only selective opinions enter it.

Hearing and not listening

The two words appear similar, but their meanings are vastly different. Hearing is just getting the information in one ear and letting it out through the other. Listening, on the other hand, is actually comprehending the information. We hear things all the time, but only when we are focused, we actually listen.

These are some of the challenges that affect our listening ability. Let's look at ways in which we can overcome them and become better listeners.

How to become better listeners?

Let's discuss eight techniques which will help you become better listeners.

Focus

Focus is the single-minded ability to concentrate on one single thing at a time. The king of the jungle is the epitome of focus. The Lion is a majestic animal. He is not the tallest - the giraffe and the camel are much taller. He is not the biggest - the elephant and the rhino are much bigger. Yet, the lion is the king of the jungle. It has got a lot to do with the attitude and the focus the lion possesses.

Somewhere in an African forest, there are a hundred zebras grazing in the fields. The lion quietly sits a few hundred metres away and focuses on a particular zebra. He doesn't focus on all of them, just one. That zebra may not be the slowest; may not be the nearest; it's the one that the lion wants to hunt. The lion though loves to play the waiting game. Not for nothing is he the 'King of the Jungle'. He loves a bit of showmanship, doesn't he? He waits and waits until it is the right time to pounce. Once he decides, he goes for the kill, quite literally. There are a hundred scared zebras running around, but the lion's focus continues to remain on the one he set his eyes on. He doesn't rest until that zebra is hunted down.

If only we could focus like the lion!

Observe Non-Verbal Clues

In the summer of 2017, on a hot and humid Saturday evening, one of my friends, Anto invited me for dinner at his place. He lived there with his wife and kid and all four of us enjoyed a wonderful meal. After dinner, during a casual conversation, we started to discuss films and our favourite director Mani Ratnam. Anto was quick to mention he had the print of the movie 'Guru' and suggested we should watch it sometime. I was a bachelor at that time and I didn't have any plans for the night. So, I suggested we watch it that night itself. I didn't even think for a second he might have other plans with his family.

Anto was unable to say no immediately. However, he came up with a weak, "Well, if you really want to, we can watch it". His body was clearly not in sync with what he said. By listening to his non-verbal clues, I got the point. It helps you decode things that are not actually said.

"You know what buddy, we will watch it some other time", I replied.

I was glad to see the relief on his face.

Take Notes

One of the simplest and most effective techniques I use to listen better at lectures is to take notes. My professors at college encouraged me to take notes so that I don't fall asleep during the lectures. Later, I realized the scientific reason behind this. If you are physically idle, chances are high that your mind goes into that zone as well. Any form of physical activity keeps the mind sharp and aids in focusing. If you stay idle for long periods of time, it induces laziness. So, get a scribbling pad and start writing what you believe are the important points.

An added benefit: You can use your notes later for reference. A lot of great ideas strike during class hours. Just take a note of it and if you feel its worthy enough, start working on it. Who knows, it could be the billion-dollar idea that the world so direly needs.

Interact and get involved

*"Nobody is going to listen unless they
know it's their turn to speak next",*

a wise man once said. How true! It's obvious, isn't it? Our teachers at school were brilliant in using this technique. They would throw random questions at the students in the middle of the class. We were always expecting the question to be directed at us. We stayed awake, even if that meant putting an extra effort.

We don't forget interactions; we only forget lectures!

You must have had long conversations with your friends at the tea shop just outside your college. You must have had hours of interactions with your mates sitting on the small walls outside your apartment. You must have talked an entire night with your sibling who returned home after 6 months from an out of town assignment. The beauty is you don't forget even one single line of it. Everything is stored perfectly in your brain as if you just inserted a 2 TB hard drive inside it to store the information. To be very honest, it is not that complicated. You remember those interactions because you were involved in the discussion. Once you get involved, your listening capacity massively increases.

If you have a query, if you need clarification, don't hold back. Just ask. You listen better directly correlating to an increase in knowledge levels.

You ask and you are a fool for 5 minutes
You don't and you are a fool for a lifetime

Silence

Most of the listening happens when you are not talking. The problem with most of us these days is we just want to talk and only talk. We just want to put our point across, have a sip of coffee and don't bother about the rest of the conversation. Well, the greatest communicators in the world are the ones who practise the golden virtue of silence. It's time to revisit a famous proverb from the 19th century.

Speech is silver, but silence is golden

This is a golden rule, especially for college students. If you are a backbencher who cannot control the urge to talk to your friends during a lecture, I can relate to you. I have done that hundreds of times. It took me several years to realize the actual learning happens when I listen and I always listen well when I am silent.

Let's play a game of combinations. The letters of the word 'LISTEN' can be rearranged in 720 different ways. But my most favourite one is 'SILENT'. It's a nice coincidence, isn't it? Well, the language itself plays a little game to tell us that, to learn something new in life, silence is the key. My dearest backbencher friends, do take note.

Get Curious

We always seek to learn things from the experts. We directly relate age with wisdom. The older the person, we assume he knows a lot. Think again. Some of the greatest lessons are actually learnt from kids. Toddlers teach us more than what the Zen masters could. The greatest quality of the kids is their curiosity. The kids never leave anything to chance. They ask a lot of questions. They enjoy learning new things. A 10-month-old baby's eyes light up when he sees a bike. He gets excited when he sees a cow. My 5-year-old niece gets really excited when I get her a barbie doll. The kids don't leave any of their toys on the shelf. They explore it to the end, even if it means breaking them into pieces by the end of it. Studies proclaim 80% of our life learning happens before the age of five years.

Don't ever get into a conversation with an attitude that you know everything about the topic. Always be open to new ideas. Have an open mind and believe the other person also knows something exciting. Most learning happens when you are willing to unlearn the things you already know. Believe me, it is not easy. But with the right kind of mindset, it is definitely achievable.

Be willing to trade cleverness for bewilderment

That way, life is more fun, isn't it? Child-like curiosity propels your listening and in turn, learning.

Work on the state of mind

You don't go into a gym and immediately start bench pressing 50 kilos. You don't start your car and touch 80 km in a few seconds unless you are in an F1 track. There is always a warm-up. The event managers know this best. They always reserve the best for the last. If you have got a ticket to watch the stand-up show of the best comedian in town, you will notice other budding comedians starting the show. They warm you up so that when the main guy arrives, you are already in that zone. The best cricketers never miss their net practice sessions on the morning of the match.

The best professors know this very well. They do not walk into the class and directly jump into the topic. They always prep you with an energizer. A small discussion on the hot topic of the day or a joke is shared before you jump into the serious stuff. We always learn immensely if we attach emotions to the things you hear. This is why learning by doing is getting extremely popular these days. Ensure you are always in a relaxed and positive state of mind. This helps you listen actively and the learnings are never forgotten.

Listen to teach

The final technique is to listen with a mindset that you are going to teach it to someone else. This technique has helped me immensely in grasping things faster. After I started my career in training, I am always looking for opportunities to share interesting stories with my students. Even when I start watching a really boring film, I am looking for that one interesting scene, which I can quote in my sessions. Even when I am watching a match that India is sure to lose, I am waiting for some last-minute miracle to happen. That would inspire me and it would be a great story to share in my sessions. This helps me focus and when I share and discuss those stories with my students, I learn more than any of them.

In a classroom, the person who learns the most is the teacher

These are the eight techniques I use to enhance my listening skills. Remember, listening is not something that comes naturally to us. It is a skill that needs to be carefully sharpened. Every single thing you have learnt so far is because you listened to someone at some point in time. Keep those listening ears open. Have an open mind and you will continue to receive the gift of learning new things. The quote by Larry King, the American talk show host sums it up the best.

"I remind myself every morning: Nothing I say this day will teach me anything. So if I'm going to learn, I must do it by listening."

-Larry King

PART
Two
THE OUTER GAME

CHAPTER
Five
DRESS CODE

When I was at school, we had our assemblies every day. Apart from the prayer song, the Principal's address and the National anthem, there was one very interesting feature in the agenda which I used to look forward to. We called it, 'Thought for the day'. This is where one of the students would share a popular proverb or a famous saying and explain it with the help of stories and examples. They were usually life lessons which hold good to the day. I still remember the thought I chose to share when it was my turn.

"First Impression is the Best Impression"

The Power of the Subconscious Mind

You must be aware that we have the conscious and subconscious minds. The conscious mind involves things you are currently aware of while the subconscious mind involves things you are not currently aware of, but can take from when needed. The subconscious mind is extremely powerful. All your beliefs are implanted in the subconscious mind. The way we act, the things we do and the decisions we make are direct reflections of our ideas in the subconscious mind. It is super powerful because ideas are planted there even without our knowledge. Things happen there without our conscious cognizance. It's human nature to judge others. It's absolutely human nature to judge others by their first impression.

People might say they do not judge others. Well, that is not entirely true. They do judge people. It's just that, they do it unknowingly. Every time, I walk into any class, I have a quick look at all the 50-odd students to get a feel of the place. I do not make a conscious effort to judge every single one of them. But here is the interesting part. Even without my knowledge, my subconscious mind forms an impression about every single one of them. The converse is true as well. The students form their impressions about me within seconds of me walking into the classroom for the first time.   It has happened to every one of us. Remember saying the below line to your friend?

"Goodness me! When I first saw you,
I thought you were a quiet guy. But now..."

This concept is fascinating, isn't it? I started to analyse this phenomenon further. Science suggests, when two people meet for the first time, it takes just 7 seconds for one person to form an impression about the other. That is less than Usain Bolt's 100m world record of 9.58 seconds!

The very first time two human beings meet is an event of great significance. The eye contact, the words they say to each other, the handshake - everything becomes much more important when it is happening for the first time. Great writers work tirelessly to create a perfect 'meet-cute' between the lead characters in a film. When the all-conquering villain meets our superhero for the first time on screen, the scene sets our heart racing. It establishes the power equation between the two characters. In a similar vein, the first few moments when a candidate meets the interviewer is of cosmic significance. It could very well decide if he gets the job or not.

Societal norms

You might argue it shouldn't be that way. You might put forward the case that one should be judged based on his abilities alone and not by his dressing sense. You might argue Albert Einstein was an era-defining genius, but he never spent too much time deciding what to wear. Agreed, there are enough anecdotes from Einstein's life to suggest he never worried about his looks. We have all seen pictures of the man with his tongue out and messy hair, but then Einstein never really appeared for a job interview, did he?

To be fair, I am on your side. I do agree one's ability should not be judged on his clothes alone. But, as a society, at a subconscious level, we do expect a fair bit of sartorial savvy (dressing sense) from people we meet in our daily lives.

Picture a patient getting ready to go into an operation theatre. If the doctor turns up in a pair of shorts, can you imagine what his feelings would be? The doctor might be the best surgeon in the country, but his dressing sense doesn't inspire any kind of confidence in the patient. It is likely the patient has already half given up. Imagine yourself walking into an aeroplane. If the pilot walks into the cockpit in a lungi, how will you feel? I am sure you will at least consider walking out of the plane.

These are just a couple of examples. The uniform in every profession has its own value. The Army, the Navy and the Air Force have uniforms that command respect. The stars in the uniform of a police officer say a lot about his achievements. The T-shirt and the cap which a player wears while playing for his country will definitely go into his list of prized possessions.

Restaurants in town are judged by the service given by its waiters. Their dress code goes a long way in establishing credibility. When we walk into a bank, we expect the manager to be wearing formals. In our subconscious minds, we have already associated certain professions with certain dress codes. You wouldn't turn up at a beach in Goa wearing a 3-piece suit. You wouldn't wear formals to buy groceries at the corner store. You wouldn't go to your brother's wedding in shorts and slippers. On those lines, it's always good to keep up with societal norms and dress formally for interviews. It clearly communicates that the interview is important for you and you mean business.

Formal dressing for Men

Shirts
➤ Wear neatly pressed formal shirts. Half sleeves are not considered formal in a corporate setting. So, it is recommended to wear full sleeves/long sleeves.
➤ Ensure you button up the cuffs.
➤ Checked shirts are not considered formal. Plain shirts are preferred.
➤ People perceive colours in different ways. Generally, light colours are the safest bet. Blue and grey are preferred. Avoid

colours like orange, brown and red.

➤ Ensure the shirt fits you well. If it is too tight, you will look like coming off the gym and if it's too loose, you will look like a kid figuring himself out at school. The shirt should always be tucked in your trousers.

Trousers

➤ Wear a pair of neatly pressed cotton trousers.

➤ Black, brown and grey are the best colours since they go along well with most of the shirts.

➤ Ensure the trousers fit you perfectly.

Shoes

➤ Wear formal shoes. Leather shoes are preferred.

➤ Black and brown are the preferred colours.

➤ Do not wear sports shoes or sneakers. Do not wear slippers or any open-toed sandals.

Socks

➤ Wear clean, long socks (mid-calf length). Do not wear short socks which come up only till the ankles.

➤ The colour of the socks should be the same as that of your trousers. ➤ When you sit down, your trousers tend to go up a little bit. It looks awkward if your socks and trousers are of contrasting colours.

Belt

➤ It is mandatory to wear a belt to interviews.

➤ The colour of the belt should be the same as your shoes.

➤ Leather belts are preferred.

➤ Silver buckles with minimal design are preferred.

A belt looks good when it is not necessary!

Never trust your belt to hold your trousers. The belt is only an added accessory to enhance your professional look.

Tie

➤ Wearing a tie is not mandatory, but it heightens your professional look.

➤ Ensure it doesn't have any loud graphical design on it. Avoid flashy ties.

➤ Solid ties or ties with minimal design are preferred.

➤ Adjust the length of the tie so that the bottom tip of the tie hovers over the belt buckle.

Perfumes and Deodorants

➤ It is essential to smell good during the interview. So, it is a good idea to use perfumes and deodorants since you might have to wait a few hours before you get your turn.

➤ Deodorants are for the body and perfumes are to be sprayed on the clothes.

➤ Do not wear very strong perfume. Inside a small interview room, it could be intoxicating. Try on different brands to see which suits you and decide on your brand much before the interview.

➤ Always keep the deodorant and perfume mild.

Hairstyle

➤ Make sure your hair is clean.

➤ Opt for a neatly combed hairstyle.

Beard and Moustache

➤ Go for a clean-shaven look or a neatly trimmed beard and moustache.

Points to Remember

➤ Always wear clean, fresh and neatly pressed clothes.

➤ Maintain neatly trimmed nails.

Formal dressing for Women

Women have a wider range of options for a formal dress code.

Indian Formals

➤ Wear a Salwar Kameez or a cotton saree if you opt for traditional Indian wear.

➤ Plain designs are preferred. Avoid anything with loud prints.

➤ Choose a pleasant colour. Light colours are preferred. Avoid bright colours like orange and fluorescent.

Western Formals

➤ Wear a pantsuit or a shirt and skirt if you opt for Western wear.

➤ Avoid wearing sleeveless shirts since it presents a casual look.

➤ Do not wear skirts that are shorter than knee length.

Footwear

➤ For Indian wear, go for a nice comfortable pair of sandals.

➤ For Western wear, go for shoes.

➤ Avoid high heels. Flats or low heels are preferred.

Jewellery and Accessories

➤ Avoid wearing loud jewellery. Do not wear too many bangles or gaudy bracelets or dangling earrings. Keep it to a minimum.

➤ Do not carry huge handbags.

Hairstyle

➤ Ensure your hair is neatly styled in a basic manner.

➤ Ponytails, buns and a well-combed straight hair look are considered formal. Ensure your hair is tied securely at the back.

➤ Avoid flashy hair accessories.

➤ Ensure your hair doesn't fall on your face.

➤ Avoid flowers in your hair.

Makeup

➤ Opt for very minimal makeup.

➤ Wear makeup according to your comfort level, but don't overdo it.

➤ Don't try anything new on the day of the interview.

If you are in doubt about having overdone your makeup,
you probably have!

Perfumes and Deodorants

➤ Wear a mild deodorant/perfume if you feel the need for it.

➤ Choose a pleasant fragrance. Strong fragrances can sometimes put people off.

➤ Ensure you have tried and tested it before and feel good about it.

Points to Remember

➤ Avoid dresses with plunging necklines.

➤ Do a dress rehearsal a few days before the interview. Ensure you are comfortable. We do not want any surprises on D-Day.

Go Unnoticed

We discussed a lot about formal dressing and how to get that killer look for the interviews. Having said that, the rules for sartorial savvy are not written in stone. Some organizations are more casual and some are very conservative. It is always better to be safe and dress up formally as opposed to dressing up casually and feeling out of place. Once you are dressed up for the interview, you don't need an expert opinion. Just have a look in the mirror. You will get a sense of how professional you look. The simple rule of thumb is,

'When in doubt, play it safe!'

Men, if you are wondering whether your earrings are too funky, get rid of them. Women, if you think your lipstick is too glossy, go lighter. Your intuition is right more often than not. If you feel good about yourself, go for it. Else, make the necessary changes.

Consider a cricket match. A batsman will gain fame when he hits massive sixers. A bowler will be talked about for his ability to bowl toe crushing yorkers. A fielder will be praised for his acrobatic catches and the direct hits resulting in run-outs. But there is another species which never gets attention. It is a very important species. It's the quiet species which nobody cares about, as long as things are fine. They only get attention if something goes wrong. Yes, you guessed it right - I am referring to the Dhonis and the Gilchrists and the Bouchers - the clan of the wicket keepers.

We never talk about the catches taken and the stumpings effected by wicket keepers. We consider those to be a very basic part of their job descriptions. But, when something goes wrong, they attract all the negative attention. It doesn't matter if the wicket keeper has taken four catches in that innings, the one he dropped will be talked about for ages. It doesn't really matter if he manages to effect two brilliant stumpings, the one he missed will take the next day's headlines. Goalkeepers in football are treated in a similar way. A hundred saves and nobody cares, but one goal scored against them and suddenly, they are under the scanner of the selectors.

Dressing up for the interview is just like the job of the keepers. As long as no one talks about the keepers, it is understood they are doing a great job. Similarly, if people do not notice your dressing, it clearly implies you have done a good job. It implies your dressing looks professional. In a corporate setting, you want people to notice you for your skills relating to the job and not for your attire. Reserve your flashy, compliment-receiving dresses for weddings and parties.

The last and the lasting impression

Ensure your trials are done well before the placements start or at least a week prior to that off-campus interview. It is very likely you won't have the time to decide these things in the morning of the interview. Your mind will have other things to think about at that time. Get this done well in advance and a major part of your interview preparation is already out of the way. Edith Head, the American costume designer who won eight Academy Awards, explained it the best.

"You can have anything you want in life if you dress for it"
-Edith Head

So, go ahead and find that killer dress that suits you. Let's go back to the thought which started it all. The first impression is the best impression. With respect to job interviews, you can safely add two more thoughts. The first impression is the last impression and also the lasting impression. As people who have seen enough of tough situations in life would say,

You never get a second chance to make a first impression
Make it good. Make it fantastic. Make it everlasting!

CHAPTER

SIX

RESUME WRITING

Communication can be classified based on different criteria. One school of thought is to classify communication into verbal and non-verbal. Verbal communication happens through words while non-verbal communication happens via body language and voice. However, there is another school of thought which classifies communication into spoken communication and written communication. Which of the two do you think is more powerful and impactful? Go ahead and take a guess because there is no wrong answer. Whatever side you lean on, there are pros and cons.

Some would argue spoken communication is more powerful. Yes, I do agree some of the great transformations in the world happened due to powerful speeches by powerful leaders. While speaking, you have the advantage of using stress, pause and intonation for making an impact. When two people are communicating using the spoken word, it is easy to understand the tone. You have the advantage of getting instant feedback.

The impact of written communication

In written communication though, you don't get live feedback. Once a message has been sent, you will have to wait for a while before you get a reply. There is only delayed feedback. But in any formal communication, the advantages of written communication easily outweigh its disadvantages. In every formal communication, written documents carry much more weightage than the spoken word. The written/printed document acts as a proof. You put something in writing and it stays for a thousand years.

The spoken word generally changes form little by little and after a thousand years, probably, it will be completely unrecognizable from the original form. Remember the Chinese whisper game we played in our childhood? You whisper a sentence to the person next to you who in turn does the same thing to the person next to him. By the time it reaches the last person, the sentence is completely different. The written document though stands the test of time. A great book written 2000 years ago has its essence unfiltered even today.

Visualize yourself getting placed in your dream company. Congratulations! You're hired! Would you prefer a printed offer letter with your company's letterhead on it or would you like a verbal communication which announces, "Hey dude! You are hired! See you next year"? Of course, you want that printed offer letter in your hands to believe you have actually gotten the job.

Remember the admission letter you received from your college? I am sure each one of you would have received a letter of admission under the letterhead of your college, attested by your university and signed by your correspondent or principal. It would have been crazy if someone from the college just called you and said, "Hey, see you on Thursday", instead of mailing the letter. It's evident when we are dealing with formal matters, the written word takes a lot more importance.

Wherever you go, the society wants to see a printed document as proof to believe anything you say. You might be the best driver in town, but the traffic inspector is not going to believe you unless he sees a valid driver's license. My uncle and aunt have been happily married for 40 years when they decided to visit their kids living in the USA. When they applied for the visa, the embassy wanted proof of their marriage. Well, you can imagine! Forty years of married life with two kids, a thousand photographs and a million memories, but the embassy still needed an official document to believe they were married. It was funny in a sense they had to visit the village where they got married, apply for their marriage certificate and then finally get it (again after producing a lot of documents like ration card and Aadhar card). I had a first-hand experience when I applied for my passport. Everything was perfect except they wanted proof I am an Indian. Well, I had my Aadhar card and an Indian driver's licence, but they wanted a document which explicitly states my Nationality is Indian. I had to get my 'College Transfer Certificate'.

Written communication is not just about providing documents and proofs. It is a fascinating concept. Let's quickly have a flashback into the history of written communication. The earliest form of written communication was done in papyrus leaves. They used nails on rocks to carve their ideas. They communicated through pictures when the letters of a language had not taken shape. After many centuries, the pen, the ink and the paper were invented. This gave way to the most beautiful form of written communication - letters.

If you are studying in college today or graduated within

a couple of years, chances are you may not have written many letters in your lives. I am not referring to the numerous leave letters you must have written. I am sure you are a master at it. I am sure you have written a lot of permission letters. When I was in my college hostel, I wrote a letter to my warden on behalf of my entire block. It was to request permission to open the TV hall late at night (outside of the regular hours allowed) to watch the US Open Tennis match between Sania Mirza and Maria Sharapova. I am not referring to these sorts of letters. I am also not referring to the tens of formal and informal letters you must have written in your exams.

I am referring to the handwritten letters to friends, family, teachers and other close ones. Those were the wonderful times when letters were considered sacred. We used to eagerly wait for the postman every day hoping he would have a mail for us. We had the concept of pen friends at that time. Pen friends are those who became friends by writing letters. Most of the time, we wouldn't have met each other. We wouldn't even know how the other person looked like. In this day of Instagram and Twitter, it might sound crazy. But those friendships were real. Every single word in those letters were soulful. I used to keep all the letters from my friends safe in my cupboard. I used to read them again and again. These days, we delete messages from our friends immediately after reading (or without reading forwards) just to avoid storage warnings on our phones.

Picture a soldier fighting for his country during the second world war. He is American and stationed in Poland. He has absolutely no contact with his family, but for the occasional mail he receives from them. Imagine the happiness he feels when he gets a handwritten letter from his four-year-old daughter which says, "I love you, Papa!" Well, if you agree life is defined by the moments that take our breath away, that would definitely qualify to be one.

When Abraham Lincoln was shot on April 15, 1865, not everyone in the world came to know about it immediately. There was no twitter or WhatsApp to share the news instantly. The news spread through the word of mouth, but people were never sure if it was the truth or just a rumour. Only after it was printed and published in the newspapers the next day, everybody believed it. Such is the sanctity of the written word. The moment a word, a sentence or an idea goes in print, it means much more than when it was just floating around as words.

After the time of letters, technology helped written communication to reach recipients faster. We had the advent of emails, SMS, WhatsApp, ShareChat, Telegram and a hundred other apps. In fact, today, WhatsApp has become so very popular that I don't receive work emails any more. A simple WhatsApp text and it's considered as an official message. Once you send a WhatsApp message, people actually take a screenshot of that as proof of communication. Hence, be very sure about anything you put on paper. It's your signature. Even before you get that much-awaited interview call, you will have to clear a step that involves written communication. In your college campus placements, even before you start to talk about yourself, you communicate with your interviewer via writing. Yes, it's your resume!

What is a resume?

A resume is the first interaction between you and the interviewer. Even before you start talking, just one glance at your resume is enough for the interviewer to form an impression about you.

Difference between Biodata, CV and Resume

Biodata

When you joined your kindergarten, your parents filled up something called your biodata. Remember the fields in that form? I am sure you will be able to recollect a few.

➢ Height
➢ Weight
➢ Age
➢ Blood group
➢ Gender
➢ Nationality

It's your biographical data. The focus is generally on personal details. Some government job applications in India still call for your biodata. Matrimony sites ask you to upload your biodata. It's an old-fashioned term. The world has changed a lot from the time the baby boomers applied for jobs. This is the 21st century and people's attention spans are reducing by the day. The corporate organizations do not want to see our biographical data during the interviews. If you are applying for a position in the police department, they do consider your physical fitness, but not generally in a corporate job interview.

Curriculum Vitae (CV)

Can you guess from which language is the term Curriculum Vitae derived from? It is derived from the Latin language. It literally means, 'Course of Life'. It is generally a detailed document which highlights your professional and academic history. Since you are detailing the course of your life, it goes in chronological order. It talks about general talents rather than specific skills relating to specific positions. It is a long document. It starts with your early achievements and the recent achievements come towards the end. This is generally used by scientists, researchers and university professors. As and when they do new research or publish a new thesis, they update their CVs to make it even longer. A CV is not something you take for your corporate job interviews.

Resume

Can you guess from which language is the word resume derived from? Want a clue? Alright, it is near England, the home of the English language. Alright, here you go, it is from French. Resume, quite literally means, 'Summary'. It is a summary of your employment, education and skill relevant to the job you are applying for. A resume is an outline of what you are and how you can benefit the company. You might be well versed in a hundred things, but each and every one of those doesn't have to go in your resume.

Personalized Resume

A very good friend of mine, Madhan owns a huge fancy store. In a social gathering, I introduced him to a colleague of mine. My colleague's kid was just five years old. He asked my friend with such curiosity,

"Hey uncle, what do you have in your shop?"

Madhan took a second before he could respond.

"We have a wide range of toys which kids love", he declared. *"We especially are famous for superhero toys"*, he continued.

'That was smart of him", I thought as I noticed the spiderman design in the kid's T-shirt.

I introduced him to one of my cousins who was just out of college. She loves trying out the latest trends in the market. Madhan told her she would love to visit his shop since he has got a great collection of fashion accessories which is fast-moving among college girls. I was amazed at the way Madhan modified his answer to the exact same question from two different people. The kid would not have been interested in earrings and necklaces, while the fashion-loving girl is unlikely to buy a superman toy.

Imagine yourself to be the owner of a big supermarket chain. Starting with a hairpin to grocery to art pieces to LED TVs, you display and sell everything. When a customer asks you what he could buy at your shop, you wouldn't give him the boring details. You will only tell him about the things he would be interested to purchase. That's how you impress him. If you want to catch a fish, you will definitely use the worm as a bait. You will not be using cheeseburgers and pizzas. You may like them, but what really matters is what the fish likes.

The exact same reasoning goes with the resume. You will have to put in what the interviewer wants to see. Too much information and it comes across as a messy resume. Too little info and you come across as someone who doesn't really have a life. It is very important to find the right balance between the two. Give the interviewer what he wants and you are more likely to get what you want.

If you are applying for a position of a bank clerk, you do not have to mention details about your biceps and triceps. But if you are applying for a position in the police department, that becomes crucial information. If you are applying for a data scientist position, the first prize you got in your playacting competition at school becomes irrelevant. But if you are auditioning for a new Netflix series, that information becomes vital. Hence, the resume is absolutely crucial to you landing your job. In fact, it is crucial to you getting that call for an interview. Hence, it becomes important to personalize your resume according to the company.

One size fits all doesn't apply to resumes

Interesting facts about Resume

Six seconds to score

Imagine yourself to be the HR of a company who is trying to find a suitable candidate for a vacant position. A study reveals that for any vacant position in a corporate organization, the HR gets around 120 resumes. Would you go through each and every one of them? The answer is obviously NO. Even if you do, how much time do you think you will spend on each resume? Let's do a simple math. If you take 2 minutes for each resume, you will end up spending half a day just scanning through resumes for a single opening. It is not practically possible since you, as an HR will have other pressing matters at hand. Studies have shown the HR scans your resume for just 6 seconds before deciding if you should be called for the interview or not.

If you are not applying via email and attending campus placements, the time taken to scan your resume is a little longer, but still very less. You might get a maximum of 15 minutes for an interview; it is highly unlikely the interviewer would spend more than 30 seconds to scan your resume. This explains the need to have a great resume. If you have a wonderful resume, in the first 30 seconds of your interview, you would be off to a flying start even before you say a word.

Profiles with photograph

It's a common myth that resumes of college students must have their passport size photographs attached. If your college has a specific format and they recommend you have a photograph, go ahead with it. Otherwise, photographs are not really necessary while applying for a corporate job.

Resume Bot

This is a mind-blowing fact. Would you believe if I tell you it takes less than 1 second to scan your resume? It sounds impossible. Well, it sounds humanly impossible. But that is exactly what is happening in reality. It is possible because human beings don't do it. Introducing Resume Bot - the machine algorithms which filter out resumes and select only a few based on the keywords you write. It takes less than a second for these bots to decide if your resume lands in the hands of the HR or not. So, if you do not have a good resume with the right keywords, it doesn't even get to a human being for review.

All these facts about the resume and the power of the written word highlight just one thing - a good resume presents you with the greatest chance of landing the job. Now, let's get to creating that wonderful logo of yours. Let's write your resume!

Components of Resume

Your resume is just like your signature dish. It has to contain all the ingredients in the right amounts to make it tasty. It should also be presented in an appealing way. We shall discuss the ingredients of your favourite dish in another book. For now, let's look at the components of a good resume. A sample structure is given in the picture.

<Full Name>
<Address Line 1>
<Address Line 2>
<Address Line 3>
Mobile No: +91-XXXXXXXXXX
Email: xxx@yyy.com

CAREER OBJECTIVE

EXPERIENCE SUMMARY (IF APPLICABLE)

EDUCATION PROFILE

Qualification	University/Board	College/ School	Percentage/CGPA	Year of Passing

AREAS OF INTEREST

COMPUTER SKILLS

PROJECT PROFILE

ACADEMIC ACHIEVEMENTS

EXTRA CURRICULAR/SPORTING ACHIEVEMENTS

STRENGTHS

HOBBIES AND INTERESTS

PERSONAL PROFILE

Date of Birth   November 12, 1984

Gender

Nationality   Indian

Marital Status

Languages Known

Passport Details   Passport No : XXXXXXXX
                       Issued at <PLACE> on <DATE OF ISSUE>
                       Valid up to <EXPIRY DATE>

Basic Information

Name

The first thing to go on your resume is your name. This might seem obvious, but I have seen resumes without names. Honestly, I have never known how to proceed when I see such resumes. Ensure you write your full name in <First Name> <Last Name> format. This format is universally accepted. If you have a middle name, include that as well.

Address

Write your current postal address. I am a freelance trainer and my current location is Bangalore. These days, with a lot of travel restrictions in place, most companies prefer hiring localities for their vacant positions. Hence, the information about your current address becomes vital.

Email

I am sure, every one of you who is not living in the stone age has an email id. If you are on Facebook or Instagram or Netflix or Amazon, chances are you have an email id. Almost all official communication is done through email these days. Gone are those days when companies used to print letters and send you by post for any official communication. Cost-cutting has become the norm for every company. All official documents are henceforth going to be sent via email. If you do not have one, make sure you create one today.

Tips to create a good email id

The Internet, email, WhatsApp and YouTube might be very commonplace for today's generation. But I grew up in the 90s (which was a fascinating period by the way). I was lucky enough to witness the internet revolution first hand. We never had computers or smartphones at home. We visited browsing centres to download our favourite posters of Aishwarya Rai in Taal and Shah Rukh Khan in Kuch Kuch Hota Hai. We created our first email ids sitting in those small cubicles. If you are complaining about the 40 MBPS speeds that today's service providers offer, we had dial-up connections which offered a maximum speed of 256 kbps back then.

I was a big fan of Sachin Tendulkar at the time (I still am) and my first email id was a tribute to him. It duly read sachin_fan@xxx.com. Those were the days of chat rooms when funny ids caught the attention of fellow chatters. Well, we all have our own funny ids, don't we? My friends have had their share of funny ids. I can recall a few.

➤ james_bond007

➤ sweety_pie23

➤ cute_krishna_92

➤ catch_me_if_you_can

They are all very catchy, no doubt. They will become instant hits on Instagram, no doubt. But, is it an ideal choice in a professional scenario? No way!

My friend Sanjana works as an HR in a small start-up company in Bengaluru. Their firm was hiring and she received a lot of applications for the position. She duly replied to each one of them informing them of their interview time slots. At the end of the day, she wanted to check the list of people she had sent emails to. Sanjana's sent items folder looked like this.

➤ terminator_arnold@xxx.com

➤ modern_bahubali@xxx.com

➤ raijni_veriyan@xxx.com

She literally had to open their resumes again to see who she had sent the replies to. Needless to say, those resumes never scored any brownie points with her. So, never create your email ids this way unless you are the terminator himself!

Why is it good to have separate email ids for work and personal purposes?

Picture yourself opening your email account in the morning. How many emails do you get per day? I get close to 50, but chances are you will get at least 20 emails a day. Here is a sample of how my mailbox looks like.

➤ Mail 1: Bill Gates is giving me $1 every time I forward a mail

(Why on the planet would he?).

➤ Mail 2: Someone called Lucky is asking me to download a friendship app to test my compatibility with my best mate (I would rather figure it out myself).

➤ Mail 3: Netflix is reminding me to continue watching a boring TV show which I accidentally clicked 6 months ago (There is a reason why I haven't continued watching it for 6 months).

➤ Mail 4: Amazon Prime announces its latest original web series has arrived (I have absolutely no intention of watching it).

➤ Mail 5: Myntra announces their annual sale of 40% on select merchandise.

➤ Mail 6: Flipkart is announcing its big billion day.

➤ Mail 7: A spam email which advises me to beware of spam emails (Ah! The irony).

➤ Mail 8: 'Kids Special' YouTube Channel just uploaded a video. Click here to Play.

The list goes on. If you have been using your email id for more than a year, you would have knowingly or unknowingly subscribed for a lot of magazines/websites/YouTube channels.

In the middle of all this, there is a mail from a prospective employer which says,

Hiring freshers. Click to Apply.

I really wouldn't blame you if you miss that mail in the sea of spam and notification emails. Hence, I recommend you to create a separate email id for your job-related emails. Subscribe only to job-related websites and nothing else. This way, you know every mail you get in that account is important.

When I was in class 12, I got an email claiming it's a lucky charm from Japan. It promised if I forward that email to 20 people, the love of my life will call me at 4 AM. Well, I duly did and waited near the phone at 4 AM. I am still waiting for that call.

Mobile Number

Mobile phones have become a part and parcel of our lives whether we like it or not. They say it's our 6th finger or the 3rd hand. Some humourists go to claim it has become a detachable body part. So, it's essential you mention your mobile number in your resume. You might argue your mobile number is something personal and you would rather refrain from using it for official purposes.

Well, if you have been sleeping all along, it's time to wake up. Welcome to the 21st century. Welcome to 2020. A lot of official communications today happen via mobile phones. You should be ready and willing to take work-related calls on your mobile even when you're on the go. You need not expect calls from your prospective employers at crazy times, but it is imperative you are available to take calls during work hours. Generally, the accepted work hours are between 8 AM and 6 PM, Monday to Saturday. The same applies to you when you make a work-related call. Never bother a prospective employer on a Sunday or during non-working hours. Always call them during accepted work hours if you want to have a real shot at it.

Career objective

It's always good to have a goal; an objective to where you want your career headed. I usually see very complicated sentences written as career objectives. Frankly, I don't understand most of them. Sometimes, when I read a few of the career objectives from college students, I feel as if I have landed in the Shakespearean era.

Most of the time, I decide to play along with them during interviews and ask them what exactly does that mean. As expected, most of the students have absolutely no idea. It was just a 'copy and paste' from their seniors' resumes.

The resume is your advertising document. It is your personal logo.

Make it unique. Make it your own. Among all the career objectives I have seen to date, the best one was also the simplest. It was written by a civil engineering student from one of the top colleges in Vizag. The career objective read as follows.

"To build roads that don't skid during rain."

It was so simple and clear I was curious to know what it was all about. He gave me a nonchalant reply.

"One of my friends met with an accident due to skiddy roads. He survived but I do not want that to happen to anyone else"

It was refreshing. Amidst all the Shakespearean scripts as career objectives, here is something which is simple, unique and relatable. What stood out to me was his honesty and the fact he talked about it with passion. Sold!

The standard method for writing career objective statements

A regular career objective statement would look like this.

"To work as a developer in an esteemed organization that provides challenging opportunities to make use of my analytical abilities and technical expertise to build attractive websites."

Let's break this down to understand better. Your objective statement must:

1) Include your goal (Work as a developer).
2) Mention your skills (Analytical abilities and technical expertise).
3) Indicate how you will be beneficial to the company (Build Attractive Websites).

This works as long as you understand it perfectly and are able to explain to your interviewer. You must know what kind of esteemed organizations you are talking about. You must be able to display your analytical abilities and technical expertise when tested. You must be able to describe the challenging opportunities you are hoping to get in your workplace. This is definitely a good objective statement. But there is one practical problem I see happening in most of the colleges. Everyone in the class writes the same exact objective statement word for word. There is one in a trillion chance that all 60 students in a class will want their careers to pan out exactly the same way!

Be unique. Make it simple and stand out.

After all, beauty lies in simplicity!

Work Experience Summary

This section is only for candidates who already have work experience. Mention the name of the organization and the position you held there. Mention the period during which you worked there. A few examples are given below.

➢ System Analyst at XYZ Ltd - 2019-2020

➢ Software Engineer Trainee at ABC Limited 2018-2019

Ensure you mention your latest experience first and then move backwards. If you do not have work experience, skip this section.

Educational Qualification

This is the most important section of any resume since it talks about your basic formal educational qualification. It can so easily be said in words, but to write it can be a clumsy affair. The best way is to list things out in a table with the following fields.

Qualification	University/ Board	College/ School	Percentage/ CGPA	Year of Passing
BE	Anna University	PSG Tech, Coimbatore	8.3	2006
Std XII	State Board	SBOA School, Coimbatore	96%	2002
SSLC	Matriculation	SBOA School, Chennai	89%	2000

It is self-explanatory and fairly simple. Let's look at each of them just to be sure.

Qualification

Always start with your latest degree first. If you are still pursuing the degree, mention it in brackets as 'Ongoing'. Start with your graduation details, move on to your diploma or Std XII and finally mention your SSLC details. Since SSLC is the first landmark educational qualification achieved based on exams conducted across the State, it is enough to stop with that. Your LKG final exam results don't really matter at this point.

University

Mention the university which issues/issued your degree certificate.

Board

Mention the board which declared your results. Eg: CBSE, Matriculation, State Board.

College/School

Mention the name of the college/school along with the name of the city/town.

Percentage/CGPA

Some colleges score the results of the students in percentages while the others score them in Grade Point Averages. CGPA stands for Cumulative Grade Point Average. Mention your scores accordingly.

Year of Passing

Mention just the year of passing. Eg: 2020 or 2019 or as applicable. Kindly refrain from mentioning the year as 2016-2020 unless you have the heading as 'Duration' as opposed to 'Year of Passing'.

Areas of Interest

Mention two of your favourite subjects here. The interviewer would like to know your areas of interest. This would help him see if you fit into the company's scheme of things. Ideally, these areas of interest should be related to the work done by the company. I recommend you be really strong with the basics of these subjects.

The interviewer knows you are just finishing your college (or just finished) and you may not be experts at the subjects mentioned. What he really wants to test is the knowledge of your basics. In my engineering, I was a student of the 'Electrical and Electronics' branch. I was no expert, but I made sure I put in the efforts to learn the basics. I learnt what a microprocessor was. I learnt the most frequently asked questions in the subjects I mentioned as my areas of interest. I got a hang of the most important circuits and the most widely used logic gates. I sincerely recommend you go one better and actually become experts at the subjects.

I have interviewed a lot of students for jobs totally unrelated to their educational backgrounds. For example, I have interviewed automobile engineers, civil engineers and chemical engineers for software jobs. I am not an expert in these fields, but I can always ask a basic question or two from whatever subject is mentioned in the resume. I may not know the exact answer for the question, but I am more interested to see the candidate's approach in answering the questions. If he manages to convince me he approaches the problem in the right way, I would give him the marks. Hence, it is important to choose the right subjects in this section. Talk with your seniors to find out the frequently asked questions in those subjects. Browse the subject in popular online forums, read books on the subject and do whatever is needed, (somersaults and backflips if you have to!) but do make sure you are really strong in those subjects. It is sure to give you a great deal of confidence going into the interview.

Computer Skills

We live in the era of computers. Every single action of human beings is programmed into computers so they could use their artificial intelligence and out marvel us. If your specialisation is in computers, you will and must have a lot to write in this section. If you specialize in computers, write about the programming languages you know, your experience of having worked with different operating systems and excel macros you have written to simplify a complex task. If your specialization is not in computers, you are still expected to know the basics.

Why are computer skills essential in today's world?

Computers have changed the way we live. The invention of computers changed life as we knew it. Men like Bill Gates and Steve Jobs had a great role to play in the transformation. It doesn't really matter what your profession is, you will need computers to send reports at the end of the day. You will have to send emails for super-fast communication. You will have to browse the 'World Wide Web' to keep yourself updated with the latest trends. I am currently using Microsoft Word and Google docs to write the manuscript of this book. I really don't know how I would manage my accounts if not for Microsoft Excel and I have absolutely no idea how speakers around the world would create visual impact without the help of PowerPoint or Keynote. Even doctors use computer software to scan body parts and make presentations during conferences.

Here is a little titbit about the advantage of having developed indispensable software. The case of MS Office is fascinating. It is not free software. We must purchase a license to use the product. This license has to be renewed every year. The cost of the licence per year is approximately Rs. 4200 per computer. Now, think of software giants that use 5 lakh computers in their offices. The company has to spend approximately Rs. 210 crores just to use MS Office. Now, multiply it with all the other companies in the world that use MS Office. You do the math. I am not going to calculate the number, but the moral of the story is pretty simple. Computers have become part of our lives. In these tough times of the COVID 19 pandemic, everything is going online. Movies are getting released on OTT platforms. My niece who is just getting into her 1st Std is getting online classes. Video courses and podcasts have become the order of the day. I am making the effort to move from classroom training to Virtual Instructor-Led Training (VILT). So, I recommend you learn how to make conference calls using the 'Zoom' app. When you get the chance, get comfortable in working with iOS and learn basic photo and video editing. Going forward, most of the opportunities you get will be WFH (Work From Home). So, learn as much computer skills as possible to boost your resume.

Project Profile

"Never judge a book by its cover", they say. But as human beings, we always have the habit of judging a book by its cover.

The title of the book goes a long way in making people want to buy it. It's no coincidence most of the great films, great books and great works of art have great titles. Take these book titles for example.

> ➤ The Monk Who Sold His Ferrari
> ➤ The Alchemist
> ➤ Five Point Someone
> ➤ Think and Grow Rich
> ➤ Who will cry when you die?

These books have great content, no doubt. But I am sure the catchy titles go a long way in these books becoming International best sellers. There are hundreds of books on personality development in the market, but very few titles are as catchy as 'The Monk Who Sold His Ferrari.' Irrespective of your specialization, you would have done at least two projects by the start of your final semester. Mention the projects in your resume and make sure the titles are catchy. It should intrigue the interviewer to ask questions about your project. If he is talking about your project, you are in your comfort zone. It gives you time to get settled and sail through confidently, increasing your chances of getting selected in the interview.

Eg:

'The role of cricket stats in performance' is boring.
'How to win IPL using Moneyball' is catchier.

Work with your team and come up with that million-dollar title for your project.

Know the ins and outs of your projects

The moment you put something up as your project, you are expected to know the ins and outs of it. It's your project and you would have worked on it for a few months, at least. So, the interviewer would expect you to know the most intricate details about your project.

In my final semester in college, we were a project team of four members - Sathish, Manick, Moulik and myself. Sathish was the most enthusiastic one. He was truly a technical genius and he could make any circuit work within a few hours. Manick had brilliant ideas. His diploma background gave him a vast practical experience. He took care of the creative part. Moulik was a networking specialist. He knew exactly whom to contact and where to get the transistors and circuits. He knew the people around town to arrange anything even if it was at the last minute. That leaves me, your author to match up with those stalwarts.

To be honest, I was not an expert at anything. Still, I wanted to contribute in the best possible way. I became the designated driver of the team. Whenever anything was needed to be procured from anywhere in town, I would do it in a flash. I could type really fast, close to 45 WPM. My skills helped the team a great deal during the submissions. Here comes the interesting part. Did I contribute to the team? Yes! Did my team members enjoy having me in the team? Yes! But then, was I doing the right thing by not getting involved in all the processes of the project? Absolutely not!

In one of the interviews, the interviewer asked me a few tough questions about my project. I was caught napping. All I could talk about was my bike rides and typing speed when the title read, 'Traffic Signal Controller'. That was a big lesson for me. I went back and the first thing I did was to call for a meeting with all my teammates. I learnt everything about my project and that gave me a lot of confidence to step into my next interview. So, deep dive into your project and genuinely enjoy doing it. It will help you a great deal. It's your project. Own it!

Academic Achievements

This is your chance to highlight all your achievements related to your learning curriculum. If you have presented a paper in your college symposium, mention it here. If you have been a member of any technical organisation (like IEEE), highlight it here. If you have been a topper in your class in one of the semesters, be proud to write it here. If you have scored that elusive centum in your Class XII Mathematics exam, share it here. Awards and recognitions are not everything, but they go a long way in establishing credibility. A committee of wise men had already declared you a winner at some point in time. This makes it easy for the interviewer to select you. He believes a man who has already been successful will find ways to be successful again in his projects.

Extra-Curricular/ Sporting Achievements

We all experienced lockdown in 2020. We didn't have the chance to go out and socialize. Millions of us found solace by watching movies, doing craftworks, painting portraits and revisiting the highlights of great sporting achievements. Yes, sports and arts kept us sane even during the lockdown. Life will be incomplete without active involvement in these two fields. Mention your achievements in these two fields in this section.

If you were part of the throwball team which won the Inter College Championship, mention it here. if you were the captain of your basketball team at school, this is the place to highlight it. If you have won a painting competition at your college, write it here. These things highlight your skills in various fields. A multitalented person is what the interviewer is looking for to succeed in a tough corporate environment.

Strengths

If you have done a self-analysis, you will definitely know what your strengths are. Mention at least two or three of your strengths here. Refer to the final chapter of this book - Frequently Asked Questions (Sub Chapter: Q3 - What are your strengths?) to get a detailed idea of how to fill this section.

Hobbies and Interests

How many of you have your brothers/sisters/cousins/friends working in corporate jobs? If they are working in a city like Bangalore, it is highly likely they would board their company bus/cab at 7 AM. When they get down at the office at 8:30 AM, all you can see is a bunch of people being dragged into the office without their will. These are the people who started their careers with high hopes, intensity and enthusiasm. After a few years, things start to go downhill. The work pressure gets to them at some point and they lose the joules (SI Unit of Energy) required to work effectively. The energy they had in college is no longer there. So, organizations rely on freshers to induce energy and excitement at the workplace.

These are times when employees of corporate organizations face severe stress. Companies plan out carefully designed employee engagement and team-building programs to motivate them. These are very expensive programs, but they do it just to keep the team motivated. If you can induce the fun element in the team and energize them, you are most welcome into the organization. The company wants to hire enthusiastic people, not zombies. So, decorate this section with interesting hobbies and interests. Some of the old schoolers fill this column with hobbies like

a) Watching TV
b) Playing Sports

These are so general and they do not sell now. The interviewer naturally assumes you are a boring individual. These days, I see some very interesting hobbies and interests like

a) Making YouTube videos
b) Creating memes
c) Creating travel blogs/ vlogs
d) Wildlife/Nature Photography

These kinds of activities are the trend of the day. In fact, most of the college students get freelance assignments in these activities. Try to make this section as interesting as possible. People tend to like each other if they share the same interests. At the same time, be honest. Do not mention something as your hobby just because it looks cool in your resume. If the interviewer actually talks about it, you will be caught napping.

Personal Profile

This section is to mention your personal details that will help the company to place you according to your strengths.

a) Date of Birth

Mention your date of birth. The date format needs to be taken care of. Some companies use the MM/DD/YYYY format while the others prefer the DD/MM/YYYY format. I recommend you use the <Month> <Day>, <Year> format.

Eg: October 31, 1999.

This would avoid all confusion with respect to dates.

b) Gender

Mention your gender here.

c) Nationality

Mention your Nationality here. If you are from India, it should be mentioned as 'Indian'.

d) Marital Status

Sometimes, companies prefer people with a certain marital status for a particular position taking into account various logistical reasons. Hence, it is recommended you mention this. However, this is not mandatory. If you are uncomfortable, you are free to skip this field.

e) Languages Known

Sometimes, the job requires you to know a certain language or a combination of languages to be effective. For example, if you are applying for the post of an English Trainer, a good knowledge of the local language helps immensely. If the company is planning to send you to Germany or France, a certification in German or

French language increases your chances of getting that job. After all, knowledge about anything will always come in handy. The dots will get connected somewhere.

If you know multiple languages, mention all the languages you know. The order is not important, but I recommend you mention your mother tongue first. I believe we will always know our mother tongue best. Follow it up with English and other languages you know.

f)Passport Details

Write your passport number along with its validity date. In certain job interviews, the fact that you have a valid passport could be a game-changer. If the company plans to send you on-site to another country, you having a passport will give you a definite edge over others. If you do not have a passport, plan to apply and get one immediately.

That concludes the basic structure of a resume. However, there are other things to take care of. The dish is ready. It is tasty and yummy. But it has to be decorated and served in a way that is pleasing to the eye. So, let's get on with building the ambience for your resume.

Fonts

Choosing the right font goes a long way in making your resume look professional. You don't have to be an expert is calligraphy to decide which font is professional and which is not. Professional fonts are pleasing to the eye and easy to read. I recommend Calibri which has replaced Times New Roman as the default Microsoft Word Font. Arial, Courier New and Times New Roman are also considered professional fonts.

Font Size

Choosing the right font size is directly related to the font you use. I always prefer Calibri and if you are using it too, I recommend the following font sizes.

➤ Name at the beginning of the resume   24
➤ Headings   16
➤ Normal Text   12

Ensure consistency in font sizes. If you are using a particular font size for a heading, make sure all headings are of the same size and so on.

Font Colour and Background

Microsoft PowerPoint and Keynote presentation software give you the luxury of using various background and font colours. However, for the best readability, I recommend using black font against a white background.

Recommended Standards

➤ Don't overcrowd your resume. Ensure you have a good line spacing.

➤ Resume must not be more than two pages (Unless you are Dr Manmohan Singh who has so many doctorates). The interviewer wouldn't have time to go through anything more than that. Don't insert page numbers in your resume.

➤ Align the margins so that there is some space on all four sides of your resume (1" on top and bottom and 1.25" on the left and right sides).

➤ Don't overuse CAPITALIZATION, *italics* and **bold** options. If you write a word all in capital letters, it indicates you are shouting. Avoid it.

➤ Print your resume by making use of a good quality printer and paper. Always use A4 size papers.

➤ Never photocopy a resume. Always take print outs.

➤ Print on one side of the paper only. Don't take back to back prints.

➤ Use consistent date formats. Refer to the 'Date of Birth' section for my recommendation on the date format.

➤ Always have the PDF version of your resume ready on your mobile phone. Print this version as opposed to an editable version so the alignments do not get messed up while printing. However, I recommend you have the editable version also handy. If you feel the need to make a last-minute change to adhere to the company's requirements, go ahead and do it.

Make it error-free

Your resume is your personal branding. You can't afford to let your brand have silly mistakes or basic errors. If your resume has spelling mistakes, punctuation or grammatical errors, it clearly implies you do not give attention to detail. Let's discuss a few tips on how to make your resume error-free.

Avoiding Spelling Mistakes

➤ Don't use words which are complicated. Use simple but effective words.

➤ If you are confused with the meaning of certain words, look it up in the dictionary.

➤ Don't mix up words which are similar and confusing. A few examples are given below.

- Expect/Except/Accept
- Affect/Effect
- Personal/Personnel
- Role/Roll

➤ Perform a spell check once you have completed your resume.

➤ After the spell check is done, read every word carefully to ensure there are no spelling mistakes. For example, consider the words diary and dairy. Both are proper English words. So, spell check will not be able to find the mistake. Only a thorough check will ensure 100% correctness.

Avoiding Punctuation Errors

➤ Make sure you use periods at the end of each sentence.

➤ Avoid using exclamation marks (!) unless necessary.

➤ Make sure every quote opened is closed.

Avoiding Grammatical Errors

➤ Don't switch tenses within your resume.

➤ The duties you currently perform should be in the present tense (Eg: working).

➤ The duties you performed should be in the past tense (Eg: worked).

➤ When writing numbers from zero through nine, always spell it out. If it is a two-digit number or higher, write the numeral. Eg: Two, 14, Seven, 1000 etc. Do not start the sentence with a numeral even if it is a two-digit number. It has to be spelt out. Try to reword the sentence in such a way that the number is placed in between the sentence.

References and Acknowledgement

There was a time when references and acknowledgement were part of biodata and curriculum vitae. The modern-day resumes do not mandate it. Almost all companies these days provide equal opportunities for everyone. Hence, the need for references has been eliminated.

Acknowledgement is a line at the end of the resume that states all information provided is true to the best of your knowledge and belief. However, it is not required to state it explicitly.

Honesty is the best policy

We have heard multiple times in our lives that honesty is the best policy. The saying takes a lot of significance in your resume. The rule is simple - Never ever lie in your resume. There are fraud organizations which provide you with fake experience certificates to boost your resume. Never ever fall for that trap. Even if you haven't landed a job, it is fine. You will eventually get there in the right path. Every company and every project you get into does a mandatory Background Check (BGC) before letting you start your work. If the BGC turns red (some fraud has been identified), it is a permanent black mark in your career and you will not be able to land any job henceforth. So, be proud of what you are. Be honest and that will definitely help you land your dream job.

Get your own style

The basic structure of your resume is ready. You know how to align it perfectly to enhance the visual appeal. The format discussed here is a very effective and proven method of creating a good resume. Thousands of students have already been successful by writing their resumes in this format. But that doesn't mean this is the only way. I am by no means bringing down your creativity.

The population of the world is roughly eight billion. Let's assume 25% of the population are looking for jobs and carry resumes. That's two billion. Do you think all two billion resumes will follow the same format which we just discussed? Of course not. In this world of imitations and duplicates, originals always have a special place. If you are good at design, implement it in your resume.

Let's study the amazing resume created by Philippe Dubost, a web product manager. He built a resume which is a near-perfect imitation of an amazon product page. He listed himself as an amazon product with an 'Add to Cart' button as well, implying he is available for interviews.

Its amaz(on)ing, isn't it? How cool is that for a resume! Put yourself in the shoes of the HR. You come across 40 to 50 resumes a day. How would you feel when you come across something as interesting as Philippe Dubost's resume? You may not decide to hire him straight away but you are sure to get curious. You would definitely want to know more about him and find out if he is actually any good at the job. Well, that's exactly the chance you need, isn't it?

Your resume is your advertisement. Make it a good one. Make it so interesting the interviewer doesn't really have time to talk about anything beyond it. It's your resume. It's your logo. Get creative and make it your own.

An original is always better than a copy

CHAPTER
SEVEN
THE D-DAY

You have done everything possible in the lead-up to the big day. The build-up has been perfect. The moment of reckoning has arrived. The day that matters is staring you in your face. It's only fair you be in the best possible shape for interview day. Let's look at a few proven ways of preparing for the big day.

The Previous Day (Day -1)
Keep your bag ready

Let's do it the traditional way. Keep a checklist of all the items you need for the interview. Take care of the simple yet very important things the previous night itself. Here is a quick checklist of the items that need to go in your interview kit bag.

1) Resume

Always carry a few copies of your neatly printed resume.

2) A file with all your original certificates

This should include your mark sheets starting with SSLC, higher secondary (if applicable) and semesters up to date. If you have other training/internship/membership certifications, include them as well.

3) Original Government ID card

Aadhar card is preferred. It is likely you might be walking into an organization or a tech park or SEZ to attend the interview. An original government ID proof is mandatory to enter the premises. You don't want to be calling your friend or asking a family member to deliver your Aadhar card to you when you are stuck and waiting at the gate. You already have enough things to take care of and this shouldn't be an added trouble.

4) Pen and A4 Sheets

Always carry a pen and a few loose A4 sheets along with you. It helps if you need to do some kind of calculations or analysis during the interview.

5) Water Bottle

The interview is not an open and shut process. There are going to be a few rounds you might have to clear and there will be many other candidates competing with you. You might have to wait a really long time before it's your turn. It's very important to keep yourself hydrated by drinking plenty of water. It's perfectly fine to carry a bottle of water to the interview and have a sip once in a while even during the interview. Ensure not to carry any other snack to the interview room.

6) Mobile Phone – in flight mode

You will need your mobile phone to coordinate things on the day of the interview. However, ensure you have it in flight mode or switch if off before you enter the interview room. The last thing you want is a funny ring tone in the middle of a great answer!

Sleep

Sleep is the most underrated therapy in the world. Most of

the health problems can be cured with a good sleep. Scientifically, sleep provides lots of benefits to our body. The brain stores new information and gets rid of toxic waste. Nerve cells communicate and reorganize during sleep which support healthy brain function. The body repairs cells and restores energy which is very much needed during the interview process. Sleeping well every day helps you be in the pink of your health. After all, you don't have to be an expert to realize good health is directly proportional to your performance levels.

Five tips to sleep within two minutes of lying down on bed

A lot of us face this problem. We go to bed, but we are unable to sleep for a long time. We try all the techniques that our elders have taught us. We check our messages and browse through social media which only increases our anxiety. We have absolutely no idea what to do to fall asleep.

Recently, I came across a wonderful video from one of the popular YouTube stars, Madan Gowri. It talks about five pro tips which the American army recommends to their soldiers to fall asleep within a few minutes of lying down on their beds. Now that we know the importance of sleep, lets quickly have a look at them.

1) Do not cover your face

Make sure your face is not covered with your bed sheet or pillow while lying down. Leave it open so you get enough oxygen to breathe. This quickens up the process of falling asleep and also ensures a good sound sleep.

2) Relax your muscles

Most of us do not fall asleep due to stress in our muscles. Starting with your forehead, down to your eyebrows, cheeks, chin, hands, thighs, ankles and feet, stretch and relax every muscle. This will destress the muscles, enabling you to fall asleep fast.

3) Keep your room dark and visualize a starry night

Blame it on the genius of Thomas Alva Edison, most of us don't really differentiate between day and night. Edison invented the incandescent lamp in the 19th century, but the human race has been alive for thousands of years before that. The human race is programmed to be active during the day and fall asleep at night. The presence of artificial light in the room has a negative impact on the quality of your sleep. It suppresses the production of the sleep-inducing hormone - melatonin, thus sending wake up signals to your brain. Hence, keep your room as dark as possible.

Once you have made your room dark, go one step further. Close your eyes and visualize a calm, breezy and starry night. It is programmed in our DNA that the presence of stars imply night and in turn, night implies a good sound sleep.

4) Avoid coffee at night

Coffee lovers, this is for you. It doesn't matter how much you love your coffee, stay away from it at night if you want to have a sound sleep. Caffeine content in our body will prevent us from falling and staying asleep. Any diet which contains caffeine is a strict no at night.

5) Stay away from electronic gadgets

Well, we are all guilty in this aspect, aren't we? We fiddle with our laptops and mobile phones after getting to bed. This seriously affects our eyes and also has an impact on our sleep. A recent study reveals radiation from mobile phones delays and reduces sleep. The findings are especially alarming for children and teenagers, most of whom use their mobile phones after getting to bed. If you have the habit of setting up alarms in your phone, make sure you keep your phone at least three feet away from your bed. This way, it is near enough for you to hear the alarm and far enough for you to reach easily.

"Your future depends on your dreams, so go to sleep.
– Mesut Barazany

The Power of Visualization

Every victory happens twice. First in the mind and then in reality

I am extremely excited to share with you a very interesting experience from a cricket tournament I was part of. One of my best friends, Raj (affectionately called as Jaffa) plays cricket at division level. He is an excellent batsman and a big fan of Rohit Sharma. It goes without saying, he loves hitting huge sixes. We participated in our company's annual sports competition and thanks to Jaffa's brilliance, we reached the finals. It was a wonderful team to be part of and we really enjoyed each other's company. We really wanted to win the tournament because that would give us everlasting memories. The matches were played on weekends and we used to practice every day of the week to stay in touch. Unfortunately, we were working on a project with a stringent deadline that week. We worked almost 16 hours a day and were able to deliver our project only in the nick of time. We went into matchday, totally unprepared and short on practice.

It was the big final. We were dreaming about it for months and it all came down to performing well on the big occasion. We won the toss and elected to bat first. Jaffa was slated to open the innings. He was the best player in our team and we obviously wanted him to stay till the end of the 12 over innings. Jaffa's first challenge was to weather the storm that is Chethan, the opposition's best bowler. Chethan had the best bowling figures of the tournament till then.

Blame it on the lack of practice, we were all nervous in the dugout. Our instructions to Jaffa were clear. "Take it easy for the first few overs and we will start accelerating from the 6th over", we said to him. Jaffa duly nodded his head, but he was not really meaning it. He had other ideas. He was in a zone which is only meant for the best.

Chethan ran in to bowl the first ball of the match. SMACK!!! What a shot! ~~Sehwag~~ Jaffa sent it high above the bowler's head for a massive six. What a way to start a final! We all enjoyed it, but for a moment, we had our hearts in our mouths. "Great shot! Great start, but take it slow brother", we all screamed from the dugout hoping to calm him down. Chethan ran in to bowl the second ball.

Here we go again and result the same!

We couldn't believe our eyes. This guy who hasn't held a bat in hand for a week has the audacity to take on the best bowler of the tournament. When we mortals were thinking of playing it safe against Chethan, Jaffa was thinking of dominating him and taking him out of the attack. The first two balls set the tone for the rest of the match. Jaffa went on to score a fantastic half-century and we won the match by 9 runs to lift the trophy and create wonderful memories (Ah! The importance of those 12 runs in the first 2 deliveries).

Long after the celebrations were over, I was still unable to get my mind off the first 2 balls of the match. What was he thinking? What if he had got out? How was he so confident without any match practice leading in to the big day? I had a quiet word with him and wanted to find out.

"I was in great touch. I was feeling good. So, I decided to take him on", Jaffa declared.

"Are you kidding me?", I pressed. *"I know you haven't held a bat for the last 5 days. You were with me all the time in front of a computer writing COBOL codes"*, I reminded him.

"I was practising every single day!", he said, much to my surprise.

"Impossible", I said. *"Unless you have been practising in your bed"*, I continued.

"Well, that was exactly what I was doing!" he said.

He went on to explain how. He loves the game way too much not to practice. He wanted to win it for us. Though he never got the time to practise at the ground, he was visualising the whole thing in his mind every single day. In his own words,

"I visualise the ground. I visualise Chethan running in to bowl. I visualize smacking him for a massive six. I have done this a hundred times in the last week. So, I wasn't exactly taking a chance there. In my mind, I knew exactly what was going to happen. I have already been there; done that!"

I was totally flabbergasted listening to the explanation. That was the exact moment I realized the power of visualization. It's practising mentally. The brain doesn't really know the difference between reality and imagination. This is why you feel emotional when you watch a movie though you know it's just fiction. When you visualize, the rewiring of neurons happens as if the incident is actually happening. If you have rehearsed it in your mind, the brain believes it has already been there and things do not look so overwhelming anymore. Practice this technique before you go to bed the day before the interview. Close your eyes and visualize incredible things happening to you.

Great theatre artists visualize themselves receiving a thundering applause from the audience at the end of their show. Football players visualize themselves scoring that world cup winning free-kick before the match (probably right from their childhoods). Politicians visualize themselves winning the election by a massive margin. I recommend you visualize yourself waking up fresh the next morning. You look great in your attire. You walk with confidence and display great body language. The interviewer is thoroughly impressed with you and finally you hear the magical three words. "You are hired!"

This exercise won't work if you do it just for the sake of doing an exercise. You will have to truly believe it. You will have to add emotions to your thoughts. You will have to actually feel the whole process of getting a job and the joys associated with it. Repeat the activity a couple more times and realise the wonders it does to your confidence. Talk to your subconscious mind. Instil the belief. Your subconscious mind is a faithful servant and will believe what you feed it. If you program it to believe you will get the job, you definitely will.

> *"He who says he can and he who says he can't*
> *are both usually right"*
> **-Confucius**

The Day of the Interview (Day Zero)

The Great Morning Routine

Virat Kohli, Roger Federer and Robin Sharma have at least two things in common. Firstly, they are extremely successful in their chosen fields and secondly, all of them have a great morning routine.

> *Win your morning, Win your day!*

Here are some proven tips to feel the morning vibes in a positive way. Great mornings translate into great days. Great days translate into great years. Great years translate into a great life.

Wake up with the sun

There is something about mornings that is calm, peaceful and beautiful. Your mind is fresh and creative. Waking up with the sun also allows your body to wake up gradually, in a natural process. It is even better when the sunlight enters your room in the morning. Your body craves natural sunlight upon waking up. This gives your body a natural dose of Vitamin D which is essential to function at peak levels. Waking up early gives you a head start over all the others who are still sleeping. This is the way nature is. However, if you are a night owl and if you are at your creative best at night, continue doing it. Waking up with the sun is a general idea and it definitely works.

Exercise

Make sure you do some kind of sweaty exercise for at least 20 to 30 minutes in the morning. This gives a lot of positivity to your mind and sets your adrenaline pumping. It helps you think with clarity and provides a spring in your step. This is your big day. For peak performance, you need peak health.

The early bird gets the worm

We all have our own styles of making entrances, don't we? If you are planning on giving a dramatic entry into the interview room like the way Shah Rukh Khan boards the train in Dilwale Dulhania Le Jayenge, kindly drop the idea. In a corporate interview, it doesn't give you any extra points and only adds to your stress. Reach the venue early. Plan to reach at least two hours before your reporting time. Budget for all the traffic and other unexpected delays you might encounter. Be the early bird, breathe in, soak in the atmosphere, get a feel of the place and be battle-ready when your chance arrives.

So far, through various chapters of this book, we have developed our inner game by enhancing our communication skills. We have worked on our body language to create positive vibes and our voice to create magic in conversation. We have learnt some amazing techniques to enhance our listening abilities and be a master communicator.

We are learning to play the outer game. We know our dress code that will greatly influence our confidence and create that professional look. We have prepared a great resume in our unique style. We have ticked off our checklists, done our exercises and most importantly visualized ourselves getting our dream job. We have practised enough. Now, we just can't wait to play the real game.

Ladies and Gentlemen, it's time to get excited.
It's time for your Personal Interview.

CHAPTER
*E*IGHT
FREQUENTLY ASKED QUESTIONS

Let me tell you two stories; the stories of two cricket world cup finals; the stories which involve the Indian cricket team. Trust me, these are sporting incidents that greatly influenced the mood of the entire nation in their respective times.

Eight Years, Two Stories, One Man

It was March 23, 2003. It was the final of the Cricket World Cup. It was India versus Australia. If you are in college now, I am sure you must have been too young (or not born) to remember this match. India had a wonderful run in the tournament. They won eight matches in a row and booked their birth in the finals. They had defeated strong teams like Pakistan, Sri Lanka and England in a convincing fashion. They were the only topic of discussion in all schools, colleges and offices during that time. They were talked about in tea shops and salons. That was the time when the exploits of the Indian cricket team was first-page news as opposed to being in just the sports pages. In short, they galvanized the entire nation for a month. However, there was one final hurdle left to reach the summit - to get past a powerful Australian team led by Ricky Ponting.

India won the toss and quite shockingly, asked Australia to bat first. It was probably the worst decision in world Cup history. Experts reckoned India gifted half the match with that decision.

Zaheer Khan was entrusted with the responsibility of opening the bowling for India. The Indian pace battery had performed exceedingly well in the tournament thus far. Zaheer Khan ran in to bowl the first ball of the final. The entire country was watching.

Zaheer bowled a no-ball! He was a youngster at the time and it was understandable. The big final had given him nerves. He had to calm down. Zaheer Khan went absolutely erratic. He bowled another no-ball in the over. He bowled a couple of wides as well, one of which went to the boundary. The Australians got off to a flying start. At the end of the first over, the score was 15 without loss. Before we could blink, in a matter of just six balls, the match was over. The occasion got the better of Zaheer. He couldn't handle the pressure and expectations that come along with a big day. If India gifted half the match during the toss, the other half was gift-wrapped and given to Australia in the very first over. Australia went on to score a massive 360 for 2. They won the match quite comfortably in the end to shatter all Indian dreams. The entire nation was disappointed.

Fast Forward eight years. It is April 02, 2011. It is the final of World Cup 2011 at the Wankhede Stadium in Mumbai. Nothing teaches you better than experience. India are bowling first and guess who is opening the bowling for India? Yes, it is Zaheer Khan. He has grown mature and is now the leader of the pack. He bowls with amazing control in his first spell and keeps the Sri Lankan scoring rate in check. His first three overs are maiden overs. How valuable is that in a world cup final?! He continues to bowl with lion-like focus. His first five overs go for just six runs. What a massive difference from eight years earlier! Thanks to

Zaheer Khan's wonderful opening spell, Sri Lanka are restricted to 274 in their 50 overs. Well done Zaheer, but the story doesn't end here.

In a very crucial moment in the Indian chase, with the match well and truly in the balance, the then Indian captain Mahendra Singh Dhoni decides to promote himself ahead of Yuvraj Singh, the eventual 'Man of the Tournament'. He calculates the chase like only a human-computer could. He controls his temptation to go for the big sixes. He is very much capable of hitting the big shot, but holds his nerve. He runs the singles hard, steals the twos in between and picks up the odd boundary when he gets a chance.

Dhoni remains calm in the middle of all the chaos happening around him. He is focused on the job in hand amidst the 43000 fans present in the stadium. He waits and waits until the right moment and just when you were yearning for a picture-perfect moment, Dhoni duly responds. He hits a big one into the stands and we all remember Ravi Shastri's immortal lines that followed.

"And Dhoni finishes off in style. A magnificent strike into the crowd! India lift the World Cup after 28 years! The party has started in the dressing room. And it's an Indian captain, who has been absolutely magnificent in the night of the final!"

Two different days, two different approaches, two different results leading to two massively different emotions across the country. Zaheer Khan of 2003 let his adrenaline rush to get the better of him. However, a much calmer and cooler Zaheer

Khan made sure he paved the path for an Indian victory in 2011. Dhoni's ice-cool handling of a pressure cooker situation made sure the victory was achieved.

The interview day is definitely a big day, no doubt. The key to win is to stay calm and composed. Get excited, but keep your emotions in control.

The idea is to know it's a big day, but act as if it isn't

Greeting the interviewer

You are all dressed up. You have had your wait and now it's your turn. It's your moment. You are about to have the most important 15 minutes of your career. Play it in your own style. It doesn't matter if you win or lose; play it in a way you will never regret later. Enter into the room with a spring in your step. Give the interviewer a warm beaming smile. Greet the interviewer with a pleasant good morning, good afternoon or good evening (and never good night even if your interview happens very late in the night) and a simple 'How are you'. Wait for a couple of seconds before you sit down. By this time, the interviewer usually asks you to take your seat. If not, politely ask him if you could sit down. Once you get the nod, get seated comfortably and brace yourself for the game. This is the final which you have always dreamt of playing.

Commonly Asked Questions

Welcome to the final part of the book. We will discuss the most commonly asked questions and ways to approach them. Remember, the interview is an interaction between two equal people. Do not think of it as the HR (In this chapter, the interviewer will be referred to as HR since we are discussing the frequently asked questions in an HR interview or Personal Interview) doing a favour for you. The HR is doing his job. The job of the HR is to find the right candidate for the vacant position. Your job is to make him believe you are the one. It's like dance, isn't it? It's a smooth waltz. You are sure to end on a sweet note if the two of you are in sync with each other.

Q1 - Tell me about yourself

Idea behind the question

a) The HR wants to simply test your communication skills. He would like to see if you can string a few sentences together and talk for a decent length of time. This skill is required to explain any idea or concept to people in the workspace.

b) It gives him time to scan through your resume when you are answering the question. So, if he doesn't give you eye contact and continues to look into your resume, do not feel offended. Feel free to continue talking.

c) He knows you must be a little nervous walking into a job interview. He wants to break the ice. He wants to make you comfortable to start with. Hence, he asks you a question for which you definitely know the answer.

d) He genuinely wants to know more about you. Two pages of writing is too short to cover an interesting life of 20 years.

Recommended answer

This is your 30-second audition. This is your chance to ease into the interview. There are different ways of answering this.

Traditional Method

The traditional method of answering this question is to have a quick recap of your life so far in 30 seconds. An example is given below.

"I am Karthick. I am in my final year of engineering at PSG Tech, Coimbatore. I love researching microprocessors and digital circuits. In fact, I am currently working on a burglar alarm circuit that gets triggered only when the home door is opened between 11:00 PM and 5:00 AM. My passion is to play chess and I love cooking. I am an excellent team player and always do my best to motivate my team members. And... I am looking forward to this interview."

The above example is a simple way of introducing yourself. The following are the things to include when you prepare the answer to this question.

1) **Name** - Yes, some people might argue the name is already in your resume. But always think from the HR's perspective. He is taking close to 35 interviews per day. Registering your name in his mind one more time makes no harm. If you have just got introduced a few seconds ago during the greeting, you can skip mentioning it again.

2) **Qualification** - Have a quick mention of your college and the degree that you are pursuing (or completed). This is especially necessary if you are in an off-campus placement drive.

3) **Areas of interest** - Without wasting much time, directly jump into your areas of interest. This also gives the cue to the HR to ask questions relating to those subjects.

4) **Projects** - If the HR finds it interesting and relevant, he will probe on them further.

5) **Passions and Hobbies** - Life is all about being passionate. Talk about the things you are passionate about. Make sure you actually talk with absolute passion. If you are nervous during this phase of the interview, talking about your passion will ease your tension. It is sure to add a twinkle in your eye, thus spreading positive energy.

6) **Strengths** - Make use of this opportunity to mention your strengths and how it will benefit the company if you are hired.

Alternate Method

There is a school of thought that declares the HR doesn't really want to hear anything that is already in your resume. So, this is your chance to impress him with some really cool facts about you that are not written in the two pages of your resume. I was once taking interviews in one of the top 10 colleges in Bangalore. I asked one of the candidates to introduce himself. I was expecting the usual, "Hi Sir, I am so and so...."

Rather interestingly, he didn't take the beaten path. He started directly with a,

"I am a National Basketball player..."

Amidst hundreds of traditional answers, I heard something refreshing. I immediately stopped looking at his resume and started interacting with him about his exploits at Basketball. There is a massive advantage in answering the question this way.

How long do you think an HR interview usually lasts for? It is likely the HR is scheduled to take around 35 interviews that day. The HR team usually runs on busy schedules and probably have to take the 8:00 PM flight back to their home towns. So, they must wrap up the entire process at least by 5:00 PM. My experience says, the interview will not be for more than 15 minutes.

In those 15 minutes, smart candidates draw the HR's attention to their comfort zone. It is much better than being asked random questions and getting into the unknown. Alright, let's play a quick little game here.

Do not think of a big black elephant in Africa!

What are you thinking now? Well, chances are you are actually thinking of a big black elephant in the African forests. So, answer this question in a smart way to attract the HR to the things you know and want to talk about.

It all depends on your personality

We discussed the traditional method and an alternate method as well. However, I recommend you choose the one that best matches your personality. If you are someone who likes to take it slow and ease into the process, go for the traditional method. If you are a flamboyant personality and likes to be of high energy from the word go, choose the alternate method. Whatever you choose, be confident and be convincing.

Even today, when I attend interviews to get corporate training opportunities, the very first question I get asked is this. Even today, before the interviews, I prepare a short and sweet answer to this question that is relevant to the requirement of the company. So, be well prepared. If someone wakes you up at 2 AM and asks you the question, you must be able to answer this with flair. Ensure you finish your answer within 40 seconds.

Q2 - Why should we hire you?

> *"... in this world nothing can be said to be certain,*
> *except death and taxes."*
>
> -Benjamin Franklin

The great Benjamin Franklin reckoned there are only two certainties in life - death and taxes. Well, I would like to add a third certainty to the list. If you are attending a Personal Interview, you can't really escape the question, "Why should we hire you?" This turns out to be a tricky question, though it looks so simple on face value.

In fact, it has become so common there are so many popular memes doing the rounds on social media. Recently, I saw one of them which really cracked me up.

Interviewer: *Why should I hire you?*

Interviewee: *Because you are hiring!*

On a more serious note, let's analyse the psychology behind this question.

Idea behind the question

If you are hired, the company is going to provide you with the resources for your professional growth and at the same time, pay you as well. In case you didn't know, life is a game of scorecards. Be it the interaction between two friends or family members or an employee and employer, there is a giant invisible scoreboard looming in the sky. For the relationship to stay smooth and blossom, the scoreboard should always be balanced. If you need something, you should be willing to provide something of value. The HR wants to know what value would you add to the organization, if hired.

Recommended Answer

To come out with flying colours for this question, you must have done a research about the company. You know the company for which you are applying for. Check out the company's website and spend at least an hour in it. You will get to know the products and services the company provides. You will know their vision, mission and values. Align your answer with what the company is looking for. An example would be as follows.

"I looked up your company's website and was thrilled to know you are planning to convert all your classroom training sessions to virtual training sessions. I am an expert at creating platforms that facilitate virtual training sessions. I believe I possess the skills and attitude required to make your company's vision come true. I am also a self-motivated and extremely creative person which makes me the right candidate to get hired."

Come up with your own unique answer. Ensure you convey

your technical and people skills through this answer. After all, sales is all about convincing your potential customer of the value your product/service is going to add. In this case, you are the product. Convince the HR of your worth.

Q3 - What are your strengths?

Strength is an area at which you are not just good at, but exceptional. This is one of the most popular questions in an HR interview. We as an Indian culture are not so good at bragging about ourselves. When we grew up, our elders have always asked us to stay humble. We have traditionally underplayed our achievements or given all credit to others. When I appreciate someone, I have listened to answers like these.

"Oh! It's nothing!"
"It was all because of the team!"

Well, humility is a great virtue to possess. We are so embarrassed about bragging about our achievements. But here, we are in a conundrum. We will have to express our strengths, without coming across as bragging. In my experience of interviewing hundreds of students, I have come across answers like this.

"I am sincere."
"I am hardworking."

These are probably the answers which were popular in 1940. But then, times have changed. If you were the HR and a candidate says he is sincere or hardworking, your first reaction would be,

"Ah! Boring!". Make no mistake, being sincere and hardworking are great virtues, but they are expected of any candidate. You can't really score points if you project them as your greatest strengths. After all, nobody is going to accept they are not sincere or not hard working.

Recently, as an answer to this question in an interview, one of the candidates told me he had good leadership qualities. 'That's nice', I thought. But I was not ready to believe him yet. I probed him further.

"How can you be sure?", I interrogated.

"I was the school captain in my 12th standard. I've had the experience of managing many events successfully. I was also the representative of my class for two semesters. During that time, I encouraged my class to participate in many symposiums in nearby colleges and created a culture of togetherness and positivity. I am currently the captain of my college volleyball team. I led my team to the University Title last year."

That was pretty impressive from him. I have reason to believe he has got exceptional leadership qualities. His achievements speak for his answer. Case sold.

Another candidate exclaimed she performs well under pressure. She went on to add how she usually doesn't study during the course of the semester, but one day before the exams, she summons all her energy to do all-nighters and pass in the exams. She didn't have any history of arrears.

"How's this going to help my company?", I wasn't willing to let it go easily.

"In a corporate organization, we will have to work with stringent deadlines. Since I can do things well at the last minute, I wouldn't panic and will come up with innovative ideas to complete the project on time. This makes me an invaluable asset to your company", she concluded.

Excellent. Impressive. Case Sold.

This is exactly what the HR expects - something simple and honest. He doesn't really want anything out of the ordinary. He wants experiences from your life that support your answer. Some qualities you could mention as your strengths are:
➤ Critical Thinking
➤ Problem Solving
➤ Collaborative Skills
➤ Innovation
➤ Enthusiasm
➤ Determination
➤ Versatility
➤ Leadership Qualities
➤ Performing under pressure

There are a hundred other strengths you could mention. But make sure, they add value to the company. Your strengths define you. If you identify something as your strength, keep working on it so that you become an absolute ninja at it. Roger Federer, the great tennis champion famously declared he never ceases to work on his strengths. He went on to add, if he worked only on his weaknesses, he would only become a well-rounded player. But when he works on his strengths, he becomes a dangerous player.

Work on your strengths. Be honest while answering this question. Whatever you answer, ensure you have some experiences from your life to back up the claim. This would help you fill-up the 'Strengths' section in your resume as well.

Q4 - What is your weakness?

If you are asked about your strengths, you can be sure of your next question. After all, theories state everything in the universe exists with its equal and opposite. Newton said it in his Third Law. In spirituality, there is yin and yang. In the practical world, there is male and female; hot and cold. So, if you have strengths, you are definitely bound to have a few weaknesses as well. It's a very tricky question. We have always grown up hiding our weaknesses. But here we are, in a really crucial situation, having to reveal our weakness. Is it okay to have weaknesses and is it okay to admit it?

Even the greatest legends are not exempt from having weaknesses. Achilles, arguably the greatest warrior known to man, had his heel as his weakness. Superstar Rajinikanth is the most popular actor in South India, but he wouldn't exactly qualify as a great dancer. Virat Kohli, arguably the greatest batsman of our generation is very tentative when facing balls swinging away from him during the early part of his innings.

Idea behind the question

The HR wants to know if you have done a self-analysis. If

you know your weakness, it becomes very easy to work on it. If you admit your weakness, that is probably the very first step in overcoming it or at least get the necessary assistance for it.

Recommended Answer

"I don't really have any weakness",

exclaimed one of the candidates. His body language was really weak when he said it. Such an answer comes across as harsh and arrogant. Such answers generally hurt the ego of the HR. After all, we are human beings and we do not like to have our egos bruised. Your aim is to get the HR on your side, not to take him on. I wouldn't recommend such an answer if you aim to get the job. Donald Trump might possibly get away with a brash comment and still win the elections, but not everyone can!

Never the Naked Admission

It is best to be honest, but at the same time don't score a self-goal by just accepting your weakness. I learnt it the hard way during one of my mock interviews in my pre-final year. When asked about my weakness, I replied,

"I am lazy!"

Little did I know it would turn out to be a big mistake. I had fallen into the trap set for me. My interviewers had a ball after that. Whatever I said after that sentence, fell into deaf ears. The interviewers repeatedly pointed out I was lazy by self-admission and they would never entrust me with any responsibility. So, never admit your weakness without attaching a positive note to it.

Combine your lessons and steps taken to overcome your weakness

Admit your weakness but tell them the steps you are taking to convert that weakness into your strength. In hindsight, I must have probably said,

"I used to be a little lazy. But that has cost me a lot of great opportunities. So, I am doing my best to come out of my laziness. These days, whenever I feel like procrastinating, I make sure I push myself to immediately start something related to the task at hand. That enables me to stay active and take the task to completion."

Refrain from giving emotional answers. Avoid talking about your personal life when revealing your weakness. Keep it on the lighter side and get over and done with the answer quickly so you get a move on in the interview.

Alternate Method

A few days back, I attended an interview for a training assignment. I have done numerous classroom trainings, but I am just starting to learn the tricks of online training. The interviewer wanted to know how comfortable I was with online training. He was particularly interested in my comfort with 'Microsoft Teams' software which I have never used before.

"I should admit I am still adjusting to the new usual of VILT (Virtual Instructor-Led Trainings). I have taken only 12 sessions so far, but I am already comfortable with the 'Zoom' platform. I am sure, given half a day's time, I should get comfortable with 'Microsoft Teams' as well." I was honest, but at the same time ended my answer on a positive note.

Some other examples of weaknesses you can mention are:

➤ Being a workaholic (Unable to spend time with friends and family, but still has a positive intonation you put your work first).

➤ Being too critical on yourself (Has a positive intonation you strive for perfection every single time).

➤ Being unfamiliar with a programming language/software/ new technology and having just started to learn it (has a positive intonation you are aware of the areas in which you need to improve and you have already started to work on it).

Understand your weakness. Enhance your skillset in that area. You do not have to reinvent the wheel if you do not find the inclination to learn a particular skill set. You just have to find the right people/tools to assist you eclipse your weakness.

Eg: If you are slow at typing, don't worry. There is software available which can convert speech into text. If you are not good at grammar, don't worry. There are certain apps available which correct your grammar and suggest perfectly good English sentences as you write. Don't be scared to admit your weaknesses. Saying, "I do not know", takes guts. It is nothing to be ashamed of. If you do not know something, look up the Internet or ask someone to teach you. You might look silly at first, but eventually, you will end up as the winner.

Q5 - What is your Unique Selling Proposition (USP)?

This is the era of competition. If you are to succeed, you will have to compete against the best. If you are appearing for placements in your college, probably there are 200 other students trying to get the same job. If you are attending an off-campus placement, the competition is even bigger. There are probably a 1000 people locking horns with you. Most of the time, organizations come with a number in mind Eg: *"I am going to hire a maximum of 50 candidates in my*

recruitment drive today."

Idea behind the question

The game gets interesting. You can't be just good. You have to be the best. You have to be better than the rest. The HR wants to know what makes you the golden egg amidst all the ordinary eggs. You will have to prove what makes you the red apple amidst all the green apples.

You have an edge if you have got something unique about you that most of your peers do not have. Be it your knowledge on the latest trends or your expertise in a particular technology or the ability to motivate a sagging team, you will have to possess something extra to tip the scales in your favour. That is the concept of USP.

Unique Selling Proposition or Unique Selling Point is a characteristic of a product/service that differentiates it from other similar products/services. If all ISPs (Internet Service Providers) provide a speed of 40 MBPS and you are the only one that provides 100 MBPS, you have an edge. If all other service centres promise to resolve customer issues in 2 days and you provide resolution within 4 hours, the scales are tilted in your favour. Hence, it is extremely important to get your own USP.

Recommended Answer

Prepare an elevator pitch to sell yourself. Imagine this scenario. You have prepared a 1-hour long presentation to sell your product to the CEO of a company. You reach the venue and get into the elevator (lift). Surprise! The CEO is present right there inside it. He says,

"Hey, Champ! I am sorry I wouldn't be able to make it to the meeting today since I got something unexpected. However, why don't you tell me now what your product is all about?"

Well, this is tricky, isn't it? You have prepared your content for 1 hour, but now, you will have to condense it to 30 seconds without losing its essence. Is it even possible? Well, considering the attention span of the general public these days, it has to be done. Traditionally, advertisements in TV and Radio convince you to buy their product in less than 30 seconds. Most of the time, they are so good we get impressed and actually proceed to buy the product. That is your elevator pitch. Prepare a meticulous pitch to sell yourself. Keep it short and simple. It should convey your biggest strength and the greatest benefit the company would get if you are hired.

One of my friends, Sharanya, recently gave an interview for

the position of a Human Resource manager at a factory. When asked her USP, she stated,

"I have got very good negotiation skills. If any problem arises with the workers union, I will be able to resolve it amicably!"

In a factory, it is not so uncommon for problems to arise between the managers and workers union. Sharanya hit the nail right on its head. She got the job.

Think long and hard about your skills. Determine what makes you special. If you are applying for a job in customer relationship management, your knowledge in data analytics could be your USP. If you want to get into your cricket team, your ability to spin the ball both ways could be your USP. If you are applying for a sales representative position, your presentation skills and the ability to understand your target audience could be your USP.

If you are unable to find something at the moment, don't worry. Build that skill. Any product becomes a brand because of its USP. You build a great USP and you will be the most sought-after brand.

Q6 - Do you have plans for higher studies?

This appears to be a very simple question on its face value, but your answer to this question directly impacts the outcome of your interview.

Idea behind the question

I have taken a lot of interviews for a corporate organization and I am expected to fill up an evaluation sheet for the candidates. While most of it is subjective, a few questions are objective. They demand a clear 'YES' or 'NO'. This is one such question. This is a clear case of open and shut. Let's see why.

In sports and movies, we have seen people performing exceptionally well in their debuts. Virender Sehwag scored a century in his very first test match. Hrithik Roshan gave a stunning performance in Kaho Na Pyar Hai - his very first movie as a lead actor. But the corporate office is a different ball game.

Since you are just out of college, it is highly likely you are not familiar with the nuances required to succeed in corporate life. That is a puzzle which needs a lot of decoding and that takes time. At the start of your career, you are going to need a lot of help from your seniors and managers. It's close to impossible for anyone to score a sixer of the very first ball they face in their corporate life. The organization that hires you usually facilitates a campus to corporate program to get you fighting fit. Once you get on the project, regular knowledge transfers happen and you get trained further. Remember, you are getting paid for it.

Popular opinion states it takes at least 18 to 24 months of work experience for freshers to feel confident enough to take decisions on their own. That is when you start paying back to the company for all they have invested on you. That is when you start training your juniors. So, the real benefit for the company is from senior employees who stick with them for a considerable length of time. If you quit the company and decide to go for higher studies within the first 2 years, it is, in fact, a huge loss to the company. A few students attend placements in their final year even when they are sure of doing higher studies immediately after college. This is a waste of time and effort on the part of the organization. More importantly, that vacant position could have gone to another deserving candidate who would have definitely joined the company.

Recommended Answer

There is one clear recommended answer for this particular question. It is 'NO'. The HR might play a little game with you at this point. He might ask you,

"Don't you want to continue learning? Don't you believe in continuous learning?"

The answer is simple. Learning doesn't have to happen only in classrooms. In fact, most of it happens outside of it. Most learning happens on the job. Tell him you will continue to learn and grow on the job. Your learning will never stop just because you don't have an official degree to show for it.

In short, in my evaluation scorecard, I will have to tick 'NO' for this particular question for you to have a realistic chance of going to the next round. If you are 100% sure you are going for higher studies, I request you to do a favour to your fellow candidates by not putting your hat in the ring. In these unprecedented times, it is extremely difficult to get a job. The last thing we want to do is to spoil someone else's opportunity.

Q7 - Would you be willing to work night shifts and weekend

shifts?

If you have followed the work culture of many corporate organizations over the last decade, you will know a lot of companies work around the clock and their employees work in different shifts. Is the company justified in making employees work night shifts and weekend shifts?

Let's rewind the clock a little bit. When the IT (Information Technology) boom started in India in the late 90s and early 2000s, the work culture of a majority of our population changed for good. My dad started his career in State Bank of India, worked for 33 straight years and retired from the same organization. I didn't know about the accounting and loans, but I always knew one thing. He would normally start for work at 8 AM and be back by 6:30 PM. Saturdays were half-working days and Sundays were always holidays. I remember the days when I used to shut down my video game and pick up a book in hand a few minutes before he came home. It was that predictable.

In the IT field though, things were different. People started with 5-digit salaries which was unheard of at the time. But it had its flip side as well. They left for work at 9:00 PM and returned at 9:00 AM. It sounds crazy at first, but looking from a customer's perspective, it makes absolute sense, doesn't it? As a customer, we expect 24/7 support for every product we own and every service we receive, don't we?

If our credit card is stolen at 11:00 PM, we can't wait till the next morning to have it blocked. We will have to do it immediately and for that, we need somebody working at that time. If our cell phone stops working, we raise a complaint at midnight and expect a resolution immediately. Traditionally, hotels, hospitals, medical stores, sanitary workers, Railways, buses and a lot of other industries have always worked 24x7 to provide us with the required services. Hence, working 24x7 is not new for us. It is absolutely necessary. I would like to take this opportunity to thank all the doctors, nurses, sanitary workers and all the COVID warriors who are working round the clock during the COVID-19 pandemic so most of us could lead a normal life. We can't really escape from shifts when we ourselves expect services round the clock.

Imagine a doctor being unwilling to perform an emergency surgery just because it is 9 PM and his shift timing is over. Imagine a pilot shutting down his engine at 9 PM because his duty time is over. Alright, I know that is a little far-fetched, but you get the point!

Having said that, it is perfectly understandable if someone is not comfortable working out of the regular hours. A mother of an infant would find it impossible to work in night shifts since she has to take care of her child. Married people might want to avoid night shifts and weekend shifts so they can spend time with their families and maintain a healthy work-life balance. Corporate companies do not force you to work night shifts and weekends, but they do expect freshers to be flexible with their work timings, unless they have a very valid reason not to.

Recommended Answer

If you are already aware of the company's work culture or seen the job description while applying, you probably have already made up your mind about working in different shifts. However, if you have a genuine reason, be open about it without getting too personal and giving too much information. Don't get emotional, but state the facts. The following are a few sample answers you might want to consider.

➤ I am single and I stay alone. So, I don't mind working in any shift if the organization needs it.
➤ I am married and stay with my family. To maintain a healthy work-life balance, it would be impossible for me to work night shifts and weekend shifts. But if there is an urgent need, I can make myself available once in a while.
➤ I am a little concerned about safety during night shifts. If you can assure me of the safety processes in the organization, I am willing to consider it.

As seen in the above examples, be open and honest about your thoughts. The safety and security of employees is of the highest priority for any organization and it is always good to discuss these things with the HR. It would also make sure there are no surprises on either side when you receive your work schedule after joining the job.

I worked as a support executive for eight years. During that time, I have had the opportunity to work weekend shifts. I enjoyed working on weekends though. My client was an American banking giant. Hence the workload on Saturdays was much lesser than the normal days. I was single at the time and used to put my hand up to get weekend shifts. The best part was I got Mondays as compensatory off. PVR Cinemas used to sell tickets for Rs 100 on

Mondays and I made the best use of it. It was a perfect win-win situation for me and my team members. These are unprecedented times when there are a lot of job cuts. So, when you get the chance, be willing to stretch yourself to suit the needs of the company, unless it is absolutely not possible. At the same time, enjoy it. Once you start having fun, work will never be boring.

When life gives you lemons, make lemonade

Q8 - Are you willing to relocate to a different city?

We as a human race always love our comfort zones, don't we? If something is going well, we do not want to experiment. We prefer to stay where we are. The fear of the unknown is massive. But then, change is the only constant, isn't it? It's incredible we resist change so much even after knowing this fact.

Idea behind the question

There might be a few reasons why the HR asks you this question.

1) The company is hiring for a particular position in a particular city. Probably, they have opened a new office space in a different city and hiring to set up a team over there.

2) The company works out of multiple locations and they need to have the flexibility to place you at any location depending on the requirement at the time of your joining.

Recommended Answer

As kids, we always wanted to visit a lot of places. We wanted to see the splendour of the Taj Mahal; we wanted to take a walk at the Marine Drive in Mumbai and we have always dreamt of experiencing the festivals in Kolkata. If you are a fresher and do not have any commitments to stay in your present town, respond with a resounding 'YES'. I believe this is the age for you to explore different things in life. Make use of this opportunity to live in a different city, learn a new language and experience a new culture. It is a lot of fun and learning.

I was fortunate enough to get placed in a multinational company in the final year of my college. My parents live in Chennai and we have our home there. I love the city so much I never dreamt of leaving the place. As luck would have it, I got posted in Bangalore. I was very nervous to start with. How am I going to cope with a new city, a new language and a different culture? Amidst all these uncertainties, I decided to take the plunge. As it turned out, getting placed outside of my hometown was one of the best things to have happened to me. I fell in love with Bangalore. I love the culture over here and the people are so warm and welcoming. If I had stayed at home, my experiences would have been limited to things I already knew. However, Bangalore was a different world altogether.

I stayed in a PG accommodation (Paying Guest) and my roommates were from Gujarat and Punjab. Thanks to them, I developed a taste for Bollywood movies, learnt a lot about the share market and in fact, developed a liking for NDTV and BBC channels. Thanks to my friends from Andhra Pradesh, I became a big fan of Mahesh Babu. One of my closest friends was from Ranchi and he shared experiences of playing alongside Mahendra Singh Dhoni in Municipality grounds. Hey, did I mention the taste I developed for different cuisines because of my friends?!

Trust me, it's a wonderful experience to explore new towns and cities. Be grounded to your roots, but always be willing to branch out in different directions. Unless you have an unavoidable reason, don't miss the chance. Explore the world. Expand your horizons.

Unless you step out of the house,
you won't even know there is a sky!

Q9 - Would you still work if you win a million-dollar lottery?

There are times in life when you want to hear the right thing. Politicians are masters at it. They have mastered the art of saying the right things at the right time. It gives you a feel-good factor and you begin to believe the world is indeed a great place to live in.

Idea behind the question

This question is asked to see what motivates you in life. Money is definitely a great motivating factor and it should be that way. Money in hand can actually be used to help others build a great life. But the HR would like to find out if there is a bigger cause that inspires you. This is a famous psychological question which determines if your priority lies in hard work or leisure.

Recommended Answer

It is absolutely fine to work for money. But it would be amazing if your work makes a difference in people's lives. Certain masterpieces created by men go beyond the mere cost of the product or service. Their value is priceless. If the Wright Brothers would have worked just for money, they would not have invented the aeroplane. If the Tatas would have worked just for money, they wouldn't have been able to touch the lives of so many people across the world. In an ideal scenario, your work must mean something more than the money you earn.

Winning a million dollars in a lottery is an awesome feeling. But you never know when the money will vanish. One thing that will always stay with you is your intelligence and the good work done using that. So, I recommend you continue to work irrespective of winning the lottery or not. Tell the HR, even though the million dollars would give you tons of joy, you will continue to do great work that makes a positive difference in this world.

Q10 - Will you lie for the company?

"It's not hard to make decisions when you know what your values are"

-Roy Disney

A man can only be judged by his values. All of us have values in our lives. Our character is defined by our ability to stick to them during times of adversity. There is a school of thought which believes executives in Marketing and Sales have the need to lie as part of their job descriptions. But that's not true. Genuine marketing agents do not deceive their potential customers by lying. They highlight the advantages of their products to convince their prospective buyers.

Idea behind the question

This is again a psychological question which determines your ability to take a stand when there is pressure from all sides. The HR is trying to determine your levels of integrity. He wants to check if you are dependable in a crisis situation.

Recommended Answer

Never ever admit you will lie for the betterment of the company (and actually never lie!). Lying is considered cheating and it never gives you long term success. In fact, it is sure to bring you down. Cheating takes the heart out of any success. If you are not winning a particular deal, it is okay. Keep persisting in the right way and truth will eventually thrive. Make sure you highlight your personal integrity when such a question is asked. Tell them you will never lie, but will do everything legal for the success of the company. This way, you can confidently tell others about the success and more importantly, enjoy it with a free mind.

Q11 - Where do you see yourself in the next 5 years?

No interview is complete without this popular question. Remember the time when we were kids. When our friends and relatives visited our homes, they always asked the same question. No points for guessing what it is.

"What is your ambition in life?"

To be very honest, we had absolutely no idea at that time (barring a few). One day we wanted to be doctors, the next day we wanted to be astronauts. During the cricket season, we wanted to be the next Virat Kohli and whenever a blockbuster movie released, we wanted to be cinema stars. We replied according to the mood that day. I don't even know if it is the right question to ask 5-year-olds. At such a tender age, with their limited experience, they would never be able to figure it out.

Idea behind the question

I don't even know if it is the right question to ask a candidate. Times are changing so fast it has become impossible to predict what would happen in the next five years. So, is it a good thing to have long term goals at all? Isn't it better to take every day as it comes and figure out a way of survival? Hold on to this thought for a moment when I share an interesting story with you.

A marathon runner covers a distance of 42.2 km to complete the race. It is physically and mentally draining to run so many miles. Even today, a lot of marathons are run on the road as opposed to dedicated tracks. The technique that the participants use to stay on course, is to have small targets. They do not think of covering 42.2 kilometres, to begin with. That would be overwhelming and there is every chance the mind would give up.

At the end of 5 km, they know they will see a tree. They run keeping the tree and the positivity it brings in mind. In the next 5 km, they will cross a lake. In the next 5 km, they will see a statue and so on. They break the entire race into small chunks and set short term goals. After all, you cannot reach your destination when you do not have one.

Coming back to our question, the answer is pretty straight forward now. It is definitely good to have goals in your career. It is always good to have a clear vision about your career. It is easier for the mind to perform when you know your target. The HR wants to know your career goals to check how motivated you are and if they align themselves with that of the company.

Recommended Answer

I have received some very interesting responses for this question. One of the candidates was very clear in his thoughts when he replied,

"I am not even sure what will happen tomorrow. Why bother thinking 5 years down the line?"

It was really philosophical and perhaps true. But, as an interviewer, I can't give any points for the answer. From a company's point of view, he will go down as someone who doesn't really plan well.

Another candidate was ultra-confident. He said,

"I want to be in your position!"

Well, not bad. But my ego took a little bit of a hit when I listened to the answer. It took me a little over 10 years to get to this position and if he says, he will achieve it in just 5 years, how arrogant of him, I couldn't help thinking.

I also hear a lot of answers based on designations.

"I want to become a Team Leader/ Project Manager/ Business Analyst/ Consultant etc..."

The point to understand here is, designation varies in every single organization. Most of these designations don't really have a clear job description. So, instead of striving for a title, try to lead without a title. If I were a fresher attending interviews, my response to this question would be,

"In the next 5 years, I see myself gaining a lot of experience in the technical aspects of the job. I would also be well versed in the business of the industry. Finally, I would be a Subject Matter Expert (SME) in my field helping my team make important decisions"

If you could see what I have done there!

a) I have clearly mentioned where I want to be in my actual line of work for which I am hired.
b) I have also mentioned about developing my business knowledge since knowing how the business works is crucial to winning deals for the company.
c) When I talk about helping my team make important decisions, I imply I would be an invaluable asset to my company (or a very important member of the team) irrespective of the title I hold at that point.

This is a very positive way of highlighting your ambitions.

"To lead without a title is to derive your power within the organisation not from your position but from your competence, effectiveness, relationships, excellence, innovation and ethics."
-Robin sharma

Q12 - Any questions for me?

Just like most interviews start with "Tell me about yourself", most interviews end with "Do you have any questions for me?"

Idea behind the question

a) The interviewer appreciates the time spent with you and gives you a chance to clarify any queries you might have.

b) It is also a test of your listening skills. If you have listened well during your interview, you will have intelligent questions to ask.

c) Most importantly, it is also a test to check what kind of questions you ask. He checks your approach to requirement gathering.

Recommended Answer

Never reply to this question with a "No questions". This is very unimaginative. In fact, it conveys you were not attentive during the interview or worse, you are not interested in the job. Always have a few questions up your sleeve relating to the job you are applying for. I was taking an interview in 2010 and one of the candidates asked me a very interesting question. He queried,

"During the recent recession (2008), almost every company laid off many of its employees, except yours! How was that possible?"

It was such an impressive question to ask. I knew this guy had done a good amount of research about my company and was genuinely interested to find out how we managed to pull through tough times. He wanted insights from an insider. This gave me a chance to speak positively about my company and we both felt good at the end of it. After all, when I get a chance to say something nice about my company, I am naturally inclined to like the person who asked me the question (who gave me the chance to talk!).

Another candidate wanted to find more about the job,

> *"What are the usual challenges faced by freshers*
> *in the first few months?"*

I knew for sure he was keen on landing the job. Extra points for him. This is your opportunity to find out more about the job and the company and what specifically is in store for you. Ask him a minimum of 1 and a maximum of 2 interesting questions.

Don'ts

When the interviewer encourages you to ask questions, it doesn't give you the licence to ask silly questions. There are a few areas which you do not want to venture into.

> How did I perform/ Will I get selected? (This comes across as desperate. Do not embarrass him by forcing him to answer such a question.)
> How should I improve? (You are already giving him an indication you didn't do a good job. If you do not get selected, you have a lot of other people/resources from which you can find out how to improve. Reserve it for later.)
> Do not ask anything personal about the interviewer. Do not ask where he is from or any other boring details. He is already getting ready to take his next interview and he is definitely not

interested in answering personal questions.

➤ Do not ask a trivia or some ancient history about the company. Questions like, "When was this company founded?" doesn't really make sense at that moment. It's your duty to have done the research to find that out.

➤ Do not talk about your benefits, allowances, cab facilities and holiday calendar. This is not the right time to talk about it. This must have been part of your pre-placement talk given by the company. If not, you will eventually find the right time to ask these questions to the right person/team once you are hired.

These are the 12 most commonly asked questions in an HR interview. They keep repeating and if you are prepared with these, you are sure to walk in confidently into that interview room. These answers I have recommended are from my own experience of giving and taking interviews and listening to industry experts. These are tried and tested answers and will definitely give a good account of yourself. However, I do not suggest you give these answers word for word. The idea of this chapter is to give you the psychology behind every question and open you up to different possible answers. Use these answers as guidelines to come up with your own unique responses.

We have discussed only 12 questions here, but if you get the flow, you will be able to answer any question that comes your way. Be street smart about answering the questions. Always show optimism while answering. Talk on a positive note. Never pose yourself as a victim. Sympathy will never get you the job. Everyone in this world has problems of their own, including the HR. The interview is not the opportunity to share yours with him. Everyone in this world needs inspiration, including the HR. Yes, the world needs heroes, now more than at any point of time in our lives. Become one!

Heroes are ordinary people who make themselves extraordinary!

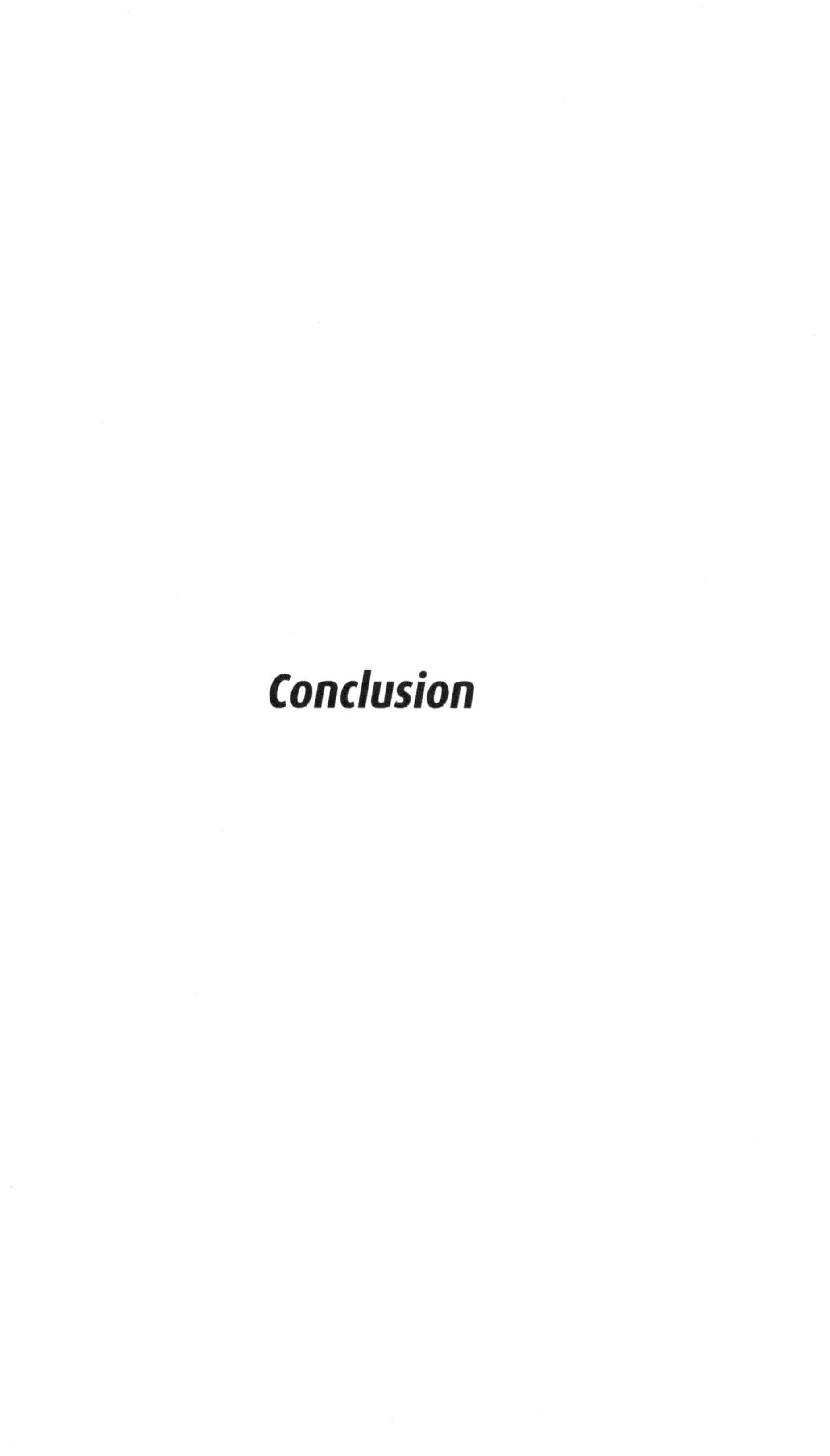

Conclusion

Great actors know they need to have a different skill set to clear an audition than to actually act in a film. To clear the auditions, they require something spectacular. You have a very limited time and you will have to make an impression within that time. In fact, my friends in the television circuit say the only criterion to land a role in a TV serial is the ability to cry without glycerine during the audition. In life, you will come across many moments which might well turn out to be auditions for great things. Be present. Seize those moments.

I believe, through the pages of this book, we have met. I believe, somewhere, at least in one of the lines, we have connected. I urge you to stop worrying and start living. As they say, You Only Live Once. The skills learnt from this book will get you ready, not just for personal interviews, but for life as well. Never leave anything to chance. Explore life and have interesting experiences. Don't be afraid to fail, but always remember to fail forward. A person falling into the water is not history. Whether he stays there or successfully swims across to reach the shore is history. Be the one who swims across!

Communication skills, body language, voice modulation and listening skills are not something people are born with. Do not believe people who say someone is born with a skill. These skills are not something you have, but something you do. You have control over them. They can be acquired if practised.

"I fear not the man who has practised 10000 kicks once, but I fear the man who has practised one kick, 10000 times!"

-Bruce Lee

As the great Bruce Lee said, practice helps you acquire any skill. Practice like you have never won and perform like you have never lost. Do not compare yourself with anyone else in the universe. You are born in this world to write your own history.

"Sometimes, it is the people who no one imagines anything of who do the things no one can imagine"

-From the movie, 'The Imitation Game'

At the end of the day, life skills cannot be learnt sitting inside a classroom. It can only be learnt by living life. But be assured it can be learnt by putting in the efforts and applying the right strategies. Now, think of all the successful people you know. They didn't get there by magic. There is a method behind the magic. There is a pattern to genius.

Right now, you are waiting behind a door. There is an unknown enemy waiting on the other side. You have two choices. You can slowly open the door with fear in mind and gently stick your neck out or you can kick the door open with all your energy and go all guns blazing. Be the one who goes all guns blazing. Load your bullets. Get ready to face interesting challenges. Get ready to face life. I wish you all the very best in your college life. I wish you crack the campus code. I wish you a great life!

About the Author

Karthick Sekar is a freelance soft skills trainer. Over the last 4 years, he has trained more than 5000 students in different colleges across the country. He has taken hundreds of sessions on Personality Development and Interview Handling Skills. His enthusiasm and high energy have helped him facilitate numerous team-building programs at corporate organizations. As someone who has interviewed more than a hundred college students for their job placements, he understands the pulse of corporate organizations and what exactly they look for in a candidate just finishing college. He is passionate about mentoring college students and gets genuinely excited watching them realize their true potential. He is a big fan of movies and loves watching cricket.

To know more about Karthick,

Facebook page: https://www.facebook.com/askkarthicksekar

LinkedIn Profile: www.linkedin.com/in/askkarthicksekar

Email: askkarthicksekar@gmail.com